RABID

Also by Pamela Redmond Satran

Fiction
The Possibility of You
The Home for Wayward Supermodels
Suburbanistas
Younger
Babes in Captivity
The Man I Should Have Married

Nonfiction
How Not to Act Old
1,000 Ways to Be a Slightly Better Woman
Beyond Ava & Aiden
Cool Names for Babies
Beyond Jennifer & Jason, Madison & Montana
The Baby Name Bible

PAMELA REDMOND SATRAN

RABID

ARE YOU CRAZY ABOUT YOUR DOG
OR JUST CRAZY?

BLOOMSBURY

NEW YORK · LONDON · NEW DELHI · SYDNEY

Published by Bloomsbury Publishing, London, New Delhi, New York, Sydney

Photo credits: pp. 2, 91, Rosaida Surman; p. 5, Patti Hayes; p. 7, Susan Hayek-Kent; pp. 8, 9 (lower left), The Sassy Pup Boutique, sassypup.net; pp. 8 (upper left), 9 (upper left and right), 10, 43, Muttropolis.com; pp. 9 (lower right and bottom), 10 (top), 25, 29, Trixie + Peanut, photo by L. Irizarry; p. 11, Karrie Martin; p. 13, Naoko Miyashita; p. 14, Shana Ostrow, handmademonster.com; p. 15, Jelena Ceslava, etsy.com: Mailo; p. 17, Erwan Fichou; p. 22–23, bestfriendshome.com; p. 27, Ruby Chan, BowhausNYC; p. 30, Kevin McCormick, obeythepurebreed.com; p. 37, Trish Aleve, Pawsome Pet Project; p. 42, thebellacottage. com, photo by Leen Isabel; p. 46–47, Alice Wang, Pet Plus; p. 55, H. Ivan Ortiz; p. 57, Dan Borris, yogadogz.com; p. 59, Irene Banzola, Faenza, Italy; pp. 62, 114, 139, Sheila Norgate; pp. 64–69, John Fleenor; p. 75, Rebecca Collins, artpaw.com; p. 76, painting and photo by James Kuhn; p. 83, Meg Price; p. 93, Matthew Sparkhall-Brown; pp. 94–95, Darial Sneed; p. 97, Annie McManus, Little GSP Photography; p. 102, ilovedogs.com; p. 103, Nicole Geller Photography for Deni Alexander; p. 106, Corey Drew, petloungestudios.com; p. 108, thatmutt.com; p. 113, Ronnie Hackston; p. 117, Gail Friedman; p. 118, Peter J. Pochylski, Builders Studio; p. 124, Tom Faulkner; p. 126, Denise Hahn; p. 128, Jaime Foran; p. 131, Michele Runje, flickr: pintavelloso photos; p. 147, David Lee King; p. 148, David A. Adams; p. 155, Anick Olmsted

A CIP catalogue record for this book is available from the British Library
LIBRARY OF CONGRESS CATALOGING-IN-PUBLICATION DATA
Satran, Pamela Redmond.
Rabid : are you crazy about your dog, or just crazy? / Pamela Redmond Satran.—1st U.S. ed.
p. cm.
U.S. ISBN 978-1-60819-837-5
UK ISBN 978-1-4088-3280-6
1. Dog owners—Psychology. 2. Dog owners—Humor. 3. Dogs. 4. Human-animal relationships. I. Title.
SF422.86.S26 2012
636.7—dc23
2012000683

First edition 2012

1 3 5 7 9 10 8 6 4 2

Designed by Elizabeth Van Itallie

Printed in China by South China Printing Co., Dongguan, Guangdong

TO MY SON JOE SATRAN WITH CRAZY LOVE

Contents

Introduction x

1. DOGGIE STYLE 1
BEAUTY 1
Spa Menu 1
CRAZY? Walking Your Panda 4
Hairstyles 4
Tattoos 6
CRAZY? Just a Little Botox around the Balls, Please 6
FASHION 8
How to Dress Your Dog 8
Accessories 10
Quiz: How Hipster Is Your Puppy? 12
How to Knit a Sweater from Your Dog's Fur 16

2. DOGHOUSE 20
IN THE DOGHOUSE 21
CRAZY? There Goes That $9 Million 25
How to Furnish Your Dog's Home 25
Fêng Shui for Your Dog 28
The Well-Appointed Dog Home 29
Going to the Dogs 32

3. DOG FOOD 34
NOT THE SAME OLD DOG FOOD 35
Dog Treats 39
And to Drink? 40
Halloween Dog Smoothie 41

Dog-Food Accessories 42

The Pudgy Puppy 44

CRAZY? Fat Camp for Dogs 45

Dogs *as* Food 48

4 SICK PUPPY 50

THE WELL DOG 51

Ten Crazy Things to Keep in Your Dog's
Medicine Cabinet 53

CRAZY? Patch the Pot-Loving Pup 53

Alternative Therapies for Dogs 54

Quiz: Get the Condoms and the Squirt Guns, Stat 56

CRAZY? Pooper Snoopers 56

Dog Therapy 57

Top 10 Reasons Your Dog Needs a Shrink 58

CRAZY? Freud's Dog Thinks You're Nuts 60

There's a Pill for That 60

How to Be a Dog Psychic 61

Dog Horoscopes 64

5. ARTS AND ENTERTAINMENT 70

DOGS AND ART TIMELINE 71

Dogs and the Visual Arts 75

Dogs and Movies 78

Top 10 Best Dog Movies 78

Top 10 Highest-Grossing Dog Movies 78

Dogs and Television 79

Dogs and Music 80

The Emperor's New Song? 80

Songs to Dance to with Your Dog 81

CRAZY? Knit Your Own Dog 82

Dog Books 82

What to Read if You're Sick of Dog Books 84

Dog Magazines 85

Fourteen Best Dog Websites to Waste a Day On 85

Dog Festivals 87

Dog Halloween 91

Dog Sports 96

CRAZY? Dancing with the Dogs 98

6 **HOW MUCH IS THAT DOGGIE?** 100

DOGS AND MONEY 101

The World's Most Expensive Dog Products 101

The World's Most Expensive Dogs 104

CRAZY? You Can't Be Too Rich, Too Thin,
or Own Too Many Chihuahuas 105

The World's Richest Dogs 105

Luxury Services for Dogs 107

7 **PUPPY LOVE** 110

THE SOCIAL DOG 111

Dog Meet Ups 112

Dating your Dog 114

Test Your Doggie Sex IQ 115

CRAZY? Seriously, This Stuff's Hard to Get 116

Dog Weddings 116

8 **DOGS ARE THE NEW KIDS** 120

PARENTING THE FUR BABY 121

Dogs vs. Kids 122

Doggie Day Care 124

Take Your Dog to Work Day 125

Helicopter Dog Parenting 125

Dog Toilet Training 127

Name That Doggie 127

Eighteen Things Every Fur Baby Deserves 129

CRAZY? Breastfeeding Your Dog 130

Toy Things 130

9. FAMOUS DOGS 134

WHAT'S YOUR CELEBRITY-DOG IQ? 135

Celebrity-Dog Matchup 137

Royal Dogs Timeline 138

CRAZY? Presidential Dog Is a Lot of Work 141

10. ARE DOGS GOD? 142

THE EVIDENCE FOR AND AGAINST 143

Dogs and Religion Timeline 143

Devil Dogs? 146

Exactly How Amazing Can Dogs Be? 149

11. DEAD DOGS 152

IS THIS GOODBYE? OR JUST, SEE YA LATER? 153

Ten Things to Do with Your Dog's Ashes 156

CRAZY? Sorry, God, But That's a Twisted Plan 157

How to Clone Your Dog 158

Quiz: Are You Crazy about Your Dog—or Just Crazy? . . 161

Acknowledgments 163

Introduction

ure, you're crazy about your dog. Your grandparents might have kept Rover chained up behind the garage and fed him some crap kibble, but you wouldn't do that kind of thing any more than you would paddle your child or dine on boiled, well, *hotdogs*.

The dog universe has changed radically since Rover's day. Dog ownership is at an all-time high, with more households including dogs than children under eighteen. Half of dog owners consider their dogs to be equal members of the family, 75 percent say they'd go into debt for their dogs, and over 90 percent would risk their lives to save their dogs.

We've become more enlightened in recent years about the lives of animals, more sensitive to their rights and their emotions, and more conscious of their importance to our well-being. At the same time, more of us delay marriage, get divorced, live alone, put off having kids, or decide not to have them at all. Which all adds up to our dogs assuming greater importance in our lives.

And so Rover isn't called Rover or one of those objectifying, marginalizing names anymore: he's called Rufus—or Lola or Max or Sadie or one of the other human names that dominate the canine Top 10.

Rufus doesn't stay home alone all day whining at squirrels; instead, he and Max and Sadie go to doggie day care, where they're fed organic chow and videotaped for the benefit of their human parents.

Behavioral problems? You take your dog to a trainer—or maybe a canine shrink.

Rufus was Princess Leia for Halloween (he has some gender issues that the testicular implants and the meat-flavored Prozac didn't really begin to address). His favorite treats are the pink, frosted martini-shaped ones, though if he doesn't cut back he may have to slim down with a regimen of low-carb food and yoga.

And okay, he sleeps in your bed, but you never let him put his head on the pillow and crawl under the covers.

Or at least that's what you tell everybody because you don't want them to think you've crossed the line from being crazy about your dog to just crazy.

The thing is, it's really hard in our over-the-top dog culture to tell exactly where that line is. Is it reasonable to bake your pooch those sweet potato muffins she loves, but crazy to turn her vegetarian? Is it normal to have your pet professionally photographed, but crazy to buy her dogcentric music—played via special dog-sensitive speakers—that you can't even hear?

To help you judge, we've laid out the range of possibilities—from endearingly loopy to scarily nuts—on topics from hairstyles to health treatments, celebrities to death. Where do you put yourself? And what about all those *other* dog people? I guarantee that no matter how crazy you may have gotten about your dog, there's somebody crazier out there. Much, *much* crazier.

The bottom line may be that no matter how far you go, it makes no difference to Rufus. Whether you string diamonds or a plastic collar around his neck, whether you feed him Kobe beef or Grandpa's stale kibble, he's going to love you just as madly. And in the face of that kind of insane devotion, can anything we do truly be called crazy?

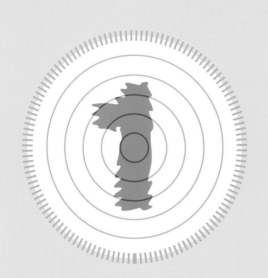

DOGGIE
STYLE

What, you're letting your dog go out like *that*? With all the new grooming and fashion products and styles around, dog owners can't just let their dogs run around uncombed, unpolished, *naked*. Pet Fashion Weeks in New York and Japan feature runway shows, design and grooming competitions, and exhibition halls full of new ideas. Here are the major canine style trends in both beauty and fashion.

Beauty

SPA MENU

Used to be, taking your dog to the groomer meant a quick bath, a session with the clippers, and a pet who looked like a newly shorn Marine but at least no longer smelled of skunk. Now, though, the array of possible treatments is much more luxurious, with real canine spa menus offering the following options:

- **Pawdicure.** Nail smoothing, pad/elbow treatment, colored pawlish, and even a glittery topcoat or stick-ons that can make your dog look just like that slutty checkout girl at ShopRite.

- **Soothing hot oil soak.** Why merely condition your pet's coat when you can soak him in a vat of hot oil? No wait, that doesn't sound good. Whatever: this is recommended for itching and allergies.

- **Anal gland expression.** Is your dog "scooting" his bottom or doing an unusual amount of embarrassing licking? Then anal gland expression may be in order, and yes, it's exactly what it sounds like. External or internal expression of the anal glands releases a substance that

WHY SHOULD YOU, OR YOUR DOG, BE THE ONLY ONE TO GET A PEDICURE? BETTER IDEA: MATCHING TOENAILS!

can cause unpleasant odor or discomfort for your dog. And really, just the fact that someone will do this for $10, the price at most salons we surveyed, should be enough to make you get it, whether your dog needs it or not.

- **Sanitary trim.** Basically, a doggie Brazilian.

- **Hydrosurge bubble bath.** Aromatherapy bath—calming scents include lavender, geranium, and carrot seed—with jet-spray rinse.

- **Deep cleansing facial scrub.** You, you probably just wash your face at night. But for your pet, a special blend of plant extracts including chamomile, calendula, eucalyptus, mint, aloe vera, and green tea can hydrate, soothe, and wash away unsightly stains.

- **Fresh blueberry facial.** So the plant extracts weren't good enough? The blueberry facial is extra gentle and, we assume, guaranteed not to actually stain your dog blue.

- **Oatmeal and brown sugar exfoliating facial scrub.** A hypoallergenic exfoliating scrub made especially for dry skin is applied to the face as the client—yep, that's your dog—sits under a gentle steam lamp for ten to fifteen minutes, *not*, we repeat not, trying to lick the oatmeal and brown sugar off her face, just sitting there patiently while the steam opens her pores and the technician, maybe even the same technician who performs the anal expressions, extracts impurities with gentle face massage.

- **Mud treatment.** Mud mask or bath treatment covering either just the face or the entire coat to nourish, detoxify, exfoliate, and soothe. They tell you they use special mud that contains jojoba, olive, and macadamia oils, which of course is much, much different from just letting your dog go outside and roll around in a puddle for half an hour—isn't it?

- **Perfume spray.** You have a wide choice of signature scents for your dog, from Aroma Organic Pawfume in papaya and coconut to faux designer brands like Arfmani.

- **Full dental treatment.** Brushing, tooth and gum treatment, tartar control. For the dog who's too damn lazy to do it himself.

CRAZY? Walking Your Panda

The trend in China: Groom your dog to look like a panda—or a turtle or a tiger. Anything but a dog. Is it happening here? At fancy grooming shows, yes, though we've yet to spot one walking down the street—at least as far as we know.

HAIRSTYLES

What do dogs have plenty of? Hair! Which makes it the most logical area for adornment. It may be as out as a mullet to clip your dog's hair close while leaving pompons at her tail and feet, but the following haircuts and hair treatments are in:

- **Hair dye.** Just like people hair coloring, hair dye for dogs comes in permanent, semipermanent, and wash out, in a range of colors from natural looking to green and purple. Use all over your dog's body or on select places: magenta ears, anyone?

- **Spray-on color.** Want to fashion bright flowers on your dog's backside? Then temporary spray-on color may be the answer.

- **Henna.** For that natural redhead look.

- **Colored chalk or BLOpens.** In case you're not the parent of a six-year-old and are not familiar with BLOpens, these are nontoxic markers with an attached tube you blow through to create an airbrushed effect.

- **Extensions.** Feathered, beaded, braided, or brightly colored.

- **Creative haircuts.** Mohawks, spikes, and fades.

- **Dreadlocks.**

- **Backcombing and bouffants.**

- **Wigs.** Long and flowing or short and spiky, blond or bright green.

- **Glitter, pompons, plastic flowers.** All can be glued on safely with school glue.

WIGS ARE PROOF THAT A DOG CAN NEVER HAVE TOO MUCH HAIR.

- **Messy.** As with humans, messy "I'm too cool to comb my hair" hair is cool. And may be had with no effort on your part at all.

TATTOOS

While there are reports of dogs themselves being decoratively tattooed—and temporary pet tattoos are available for that edgy night on the town—most dog owners find the practice unethical. The animal has to be sedated, which carries its own dangers, and has no desire to be tattooed.

The exceptions are identification tattoos, which many breeders use

CRAZY? Just a Little Botox around the Balls, Please

While the Humane Society opposes surgery done for purely cosmetic reasons and the American Kennel Club bans physically altered dogs from competition, there is one area where dog cosmetic surgery is catching on: testicular implants.

You heard right. The idea is that ball implants will bolster Buddy's self-esteem after neutering and make him feel just like the other dogs. And lest you think this is a publicity stunt, the manufacturer of Neuticles, which cost nearly $100, claims to have sold a quarter million pairs so far.

Most of the other canine plastic surgery performed today has a medical rationale, such as rhinoplasty on short-nosed dogs to relieve breathing problems, chin lifts on mastiffs to relieve drooling problems, and fold tucks for bulldogs around the eyes, cheeks, and vulva to relieve—oh God, please don't tell me.

Breast reductions are not unheard of, but again, usually are done for a health reason such as excessive sagging due to pregnancy or deformity due to overbreeding.

The exception: Brazil, where even I could afford a facelift. Canine plastic surgeons there do everything from Restylane for crooked ears to Botox for wrinkles. (Wait: dogs get wrinkles?) But São Paulo surgeon Dr. Edgard Brito has his limits: "I would never," he has been quoted as saying, "attach an artificial testicle."

along with microchips to identify dogs in case they're lost or stolen, and tattoos done for health reasons, as when a vet tattoos a dog's nose black to protect it from the sun.

But dogs are a popular subject for human tattoos: a Yorkie across the back of the neck, a smiling Lab on the calf, or maybe a stylized mythological dog curling around a bicep . . .

YOU'LL NEVER HAVE TO MISS YOUR DOG'S FACE IF YOU HAVE IT TATTOOED ON YOUR LEG.

Fashion

HOW TO DRESS YOUR DOG

What, you just let your dog walk around naked? There's no excuse for that, especially when you could dress him or her in one of these amazing fashion items:

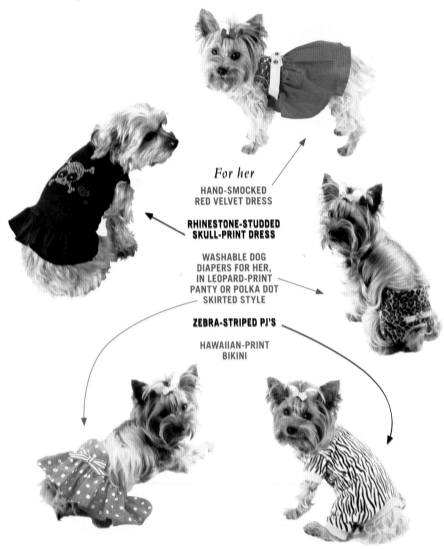

For her

HAND-SMOCKED
RED VELVET DRESS

**RHINESTONE-STUDDED
SKULL-PRINT DRESS**

WASHABLE DOG
DIAPERS FOR HER,
IN LEOPARD-PRINT
PANTY OR POLKA DOT
SKIRTED STYLE

ZEBRA-STRIPED PJ'S

HAWAIIAN-PRINT
BIKINI

For him

REVERSIBLE LEOPARD
PUFFER VEST

**GREEN BAY PACKER
FLEECE VEST**

ALPACA FAIR ISLE–
PATTERNED KNIT
SWEATER

**VINTAGE
BOY SCOUT SHIRT**

DEVIL HOODIE
WITH HORNS SEWN
ONTO THE HOOD

**VELOUR SWEAT SUIT
FOR YOUR LEISURE
ANIMAL, WITH
KANGAROO POCKET
AND ELASTIC PANTS
SUITABLE FOR
TOILETING**

BROCADE TUXEDO
VEST—WITH FESTIVE
BOW TIE

CLASSIC TOGGLE COAT

Accessories

NONSKID DOG SOCKS

RUBY SLIPPERS,
FOUR TO A PACK

**CANVAS HIGH-TOPS
WITH FAUX LACES**

BONE-SHAPED CHARM
THAT SPELLS OUT
"DIVA" OR "STUD"
IN RHINESTONES

**DOG COLLAR WITH
CROSS OR STAR OF DAVID**

MAGNETIC FAKE
DIAMOND STUD EARRINGS

**DOUBLE-STRAND PINK
PEARL NECKLACE**

DOGGLES—K9 OPTICS
SUNGLASSES WITH
RHINESTONE HEART OR
PAW PRINT DETAIL—AS
SEEN IN *BEVERLY HILLS
CHIHUAHUA*

**BANDANNA THAT SAYS
"BITCH MAGNET"**

STRAW BONNET WITH FAUX
FLOWERS AND LACE

**LED SPORTS CAP THAT
READS "FOOTBALL,"
"BASEBALL," OR "SOCCER"
AND LIGHTS UP TO MAKE
YOUR DOG EASIER TO FIND
IN THE DARK**

HYDRATION BACKPACK
THAT INCLUDES TWO
REFILLABLE WATER
POUCHES—ONE FOR YOUR
DOG AND ONE FOR YOU!

WAIT A MINUTE. WHAT ARE THESE FRONT TWO SHOES FOR?

How Hipster Is Your Puppy?

Do you want your puppy to be a hipster? You do? Okay, then you've probably failed before you even start. Being a hipster is all about not wanting to be a hipster, and wanting to be a hipster pretty much guarantees you'll never be one. Not really. Got it?

Good.

That said, the whole so-uncool-it's-cool thing pretty much means that the only way to be truly cool is to be truly, truly uncool, which means that the coolest thing you can do is to try to be cool. And yes, we're absolutely sure that's clear.

But if you still need definition on exactly how hipster your pup is, take this simple quiz:

How ugly is your dog?

a. My dog is so ugly that the shelter was about to euthanize him because they thought no one would ever be crazy enough to adopt him.

b. My dog is so ugly that people say she's cute because they're way too embarrassed to say what they really think.

c. My dog is adorable.

What kind of glasses does your dog wear?

a. Neon-framed sunglasses.

b. Heavy horn-rimmed glasses that make him look like an intellectual, but only when being photographed.

c. Glasses? Why would my dog wear glasses?

What kind of hat does your dog wear?

a. Vintage porkpie, just like mine.

b. Stocking cap from A.P.C. just like mine, that I tore little holes in so it would look like a moth-eaten one from Goodwill.

c. Hat? Why would my dog wear a hat?

What is your dog's name?

a. Karen or Bob, one of those midcentury names.

b. Sheldon or Sadie, one of those old-people names.

c. Buster or Bowser, one of those dog names.

Where does your dog hang out?

a. McCarren Park in Brooklyn.

b. Dolores Park in San Francisco.

c. At home in Ohio.

What is your dog's favorite sport?

a. Skateboarding.

b. Surfing.

c. Frisbee playing.

What does your dog like to eat?

a. Karen is a vegan.

b. Sheldon eats only organic food, except for the occasional hotdog consumed ironically on the boardwalk at Rockaway.

c. Buster is happy with a scoop of kibble.

Does your dog have any famous friends?

a. At Occupy Wall Street, Bob got petted by Kanye.

b. At Opening Ceremony, Sadie went into the fitting room with Jason Schwartzman.

c. They haven't actually met, but I think Bowser has a crush on Jessica Simpson.

Key:

a. If you answered mostly *a*'s, your dog is definitely a hipster, but perhaps you're trying a little too hard and you're a little too hip? Final judgment: Not hipster.

b. If you answered mostly *b*'s, your dog is also definitely a hipster, but again, it seems as if you might be trying a bit too hard and acting a smidge too hip. Sorry, therefore not hipster either.

c. You are totally not hip or a hipster. Therefore, you might be a hipster. But who cares?

COZY AND SEXY.

HOW TO KNIT A SWEATER FROM YOUR DOG'S FUR IN SEVENTEEN SIMPLE STEPS

Do you wear sweaters that are all covered in dog hair? That's nuthin'. *Real* dog lovers wear sweaters made from dog hair. You can create a dog-hair sweater yourself, in your own home, in as much time as it takes to, oh, produce a dog show for Animal Planet or give birth to a couple of generations of puppies.

Here's how:

1. Brush your dog or at least the corpse of your dog. Brush the soft long under hair from the back, sides, and belly of your dog; stiff guard hairs or the stuff that ends up in the vacuum cleaner won't do. It's preferable to make your sweater from the hair of a live dog, for reasons that will soon become obvious if they're not so already. But if the sweater-making idea doesn't occur to you until after your dog dies, all is not lost, provided you have not already buried or cremated your dog.

2. Store the hair in a paper bag or clean white pillowcase—plastic will mat it—until you have enough to make a sweater (about a pillowcase full). Or at least a scarf. Or at least until you find it in the back of the closet, scream in horror, and throw it out before you remember what it is.

3. Add cedar chips or herbs like rosemary, thyme, and cloves to keep the moths away from stored hair. No mothballs because then your dog hair will smell even worse than it already does.

4. Wash the dog hair with a mild shampoo and lay it out to dry. If it still smells like dog, wash it a few more times.

IF THE DOG'S COAT
AND THE DOG OWNER'S
SWEATER ARE LOOK-
ALIKES, THAT'S NO
ACCIDENT.

5. Card the dog hair to prepare for spinning. No, I don't know what this means either.

6. Spin the dog hair into yarn. Or maybe, if you're really talented, into gold. At which point you'll get to marry a prince and go live near a military base in Wales.

7. If you're not macha enough to spin your own yarn, contract with VIP Fibers to do it for you.

8. Wonder whether, if you worked at McDonald's for the amount of time it's taking you to do all this, you could have just bought yourself a nice cashmere sweater.

9. Wash yarn. Why again? Have you smelled your dog lately?

10. Knit loosely, breaking—not cutting—dog-hair yarn, and joining with overlaps, never knots. Otherwise, you'll end up with a garment that looks like it was knit from, you know, dog hair.

11. Go somewhere wearing your dog-hair sweater, preferably with your dog. Note: Not recommended if your dog is dead.

12. Wait for someone to admire your sweater.

13. Go ahead, keep waiting.

14. Mistaking the question on where you got your sweater for a compliment, exclaim that you made it yourself! From your dog's hair!

15. Do not chase the person when he backs away.

16. Do not overcompensate by telling even more people that you knit the sweater from your dog's fur.

17. Oh, yeah, and when you get home, better **wash it again.**

CRAZY about your dog	Just CRAZY
Buying your pet a cute little outfit for Halloween so he doesn't feel left out at the dog park.	Spending so much time constructing your dog's costume you forget to buy candy for the trick-or-treaters.
Dyeing that fluffy patch at the top of her head hot pink.	Touching up her roots.
Protecting him with a waterproof coat when you walk in the rain.	Accessorizing his raincoat with rubber boots and a head-mounted umbrella

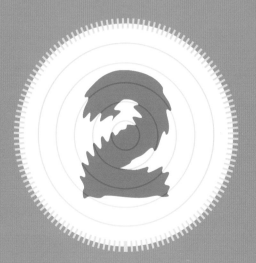

DOG
HOUSE

In the Doghouse

Nobody wants to be in the doghouse, not even the dog.

And when doghouses were a few nailed-together boards over a dirt floor, who could blame them?

Now, doghouse manufacturers and designers are seeking to change all that with new doghouses that combine high design with canine comfort. Or at least the illusion of it. The state of doghouse architecture now:

Doghouses better than your house. A two-bedroom manse in Britain designed by a prominent architect has a $250,000 sound system, 52-inch plasma TV, and retina-scanning security entry.

Royal doghouses. A Japanese dog lover spent six months creating a replica of the sixteenth-century Matsumoto Castle for his pet.

Mini-me doghouses. Paris Hilton built a house for her dogs modeled on her own California-style mansion. It includes Philippe Starck furniture, a black crystal chandelier, and of course, a closet.

Suburban doghouses. Doghouses modeled on Victorians, Cape Cods, or log cabins are widely available for $2,000 to $3,000 and come equipped with shuttered windows, flower boxes, gingerbread trim, front porches, and stairways to rooftop (you'll pardon the expression) catwalks. For another $600 or so, you can even install a remote-controlled heating and air-conditioning unit.

GERMAN *HUNDEHÄUSER* IN THE
BAUHAUS STYLE EVIDENCES
EUROPEAN CHIC.

European doghouses. In Europe, where everything is cooler, a German company at bestfriendshome.com makes one *Hundehäuser* in the Bauhaus style and another that resembles Scarlett O'Hara's home plantation Tara. Italian designer Marco Morosini, who claims to be "creating temples for four-legged gods," sells his glass house, Buddhist temple, and doggie mobile home resembling an Airstream from the site dogisagod.it.

Sustainable doghouses. Nice idea, but one company that produced a doghouse with plants growing out of its roof has gone out of business. And a molded plastic doghouse that you bury in your backyard claims to be naturally heated and cooled by the earth but might make you feel not like a green crusader so much as a kidnapper hiding his prey in an underground pit.

Indoor doghouses. Some forward-thinking and practical designers seem to realize that modern dogs have no intention of sleeping outside, no matter how chic the house, and have instead created indoor doghouses. These include a portable folding doghouse as well as end tables and rocking chairs that harbor doghouse-like enclosures.

Virtual doghouses. And then there are the life-size doghouse decals to paste on your wall, a nod to the notion of an old-school doghouse while at the same time acknowledging the reality that your house now *is* the doghouse. At least your dog lets you live there, too.

HOW TO FURNISH YOUR DOG'S HOME

Why let your dog sleep on your bed or curl up in your favorite chair when he can have his own furniture? Every doghouse can use the following items:

Louis XVI four-poster canopy bed, $4,538. With fully lined, plaid tapestry curtains, removable for dry cleaning.

Faux-fur bed shaped like a car or boat, $249 from Trixie + Peanut. For the animal who likes to be in the driver's seat.

Tempur-Pedic mattress, $425 for extra large. If you're still sleeping on foam, you may want to curl up next to your dog.

Sweetcake dog bed, $212. Dutch-designed plastic dog bed that looks like a cupcake wrapper.

Italian Renaissance sofa, $785. Tapestry upholstered.

Zebra-print Victorian chaise longue, $299. Suitable for fainting.

Contemporary conversation pit, $359. Sleek gray-and-black sofa that can accommodate several small dogs in conversation pit style.

Designer pod chair, $598. C-shaped bent-plywood "Eames chair for your dog" with choice of five veneer finishes and faux-collie fur pad.

Wildebeest pet rug, $49. Shaggy fleece rug from Etsy.

Feminine armoire, $259. White-and-pink armoire with three adjustable hanging racks, drawer, and doors with bone-shaped windows.

Decorator fabric crate cover, $96. Crates may be practical, but you don't want your darling doggie to feel like you're putting her in a *cage*, do you? A crate cover in chic cabana stripes or toile masks those grim realities for fur babies and parents alike.

FÊNG SHUI FOR YOUR DOG

When you bring a new puppy home, what's the first thing you should do to your house?

Fêng shui it to make it a hospitable place for your new dog, of course!

DeAnna Radaj is a fêng shui expert in Charlotte, North Carolina, who's consulted with many pet owners on applying fêng shui principles to create a dog-friendly home.

If you'd rather spend your pet budget on, say, little rubber underpants, how can you doggie fêng shui your house yourself? Radaj's tips:

Declutter the entryway. "It's all about energy," says Radaj. Starting at the front door, you (and your dog) want to be able to walk easily and freely into the house without slamming into furniture, stepping over clutter, getting confused.

Place the food bowl in the power position. Ideal: in the far corner of the room diagonal to and facing the entryway, the most psychologically secure position for dogs or people. You don't want your dog to have his head in the corner and his back exposed.

Place the bed in the power position. Same basic principle as the food bowl, ideally in a quiet corner. Never place the bed directly in line with the door, which is the death position.

Give your pet his own bed. "With fêng shui you want something soft, like Sherpa wool, and free-flowing organic lines that help induce sleep," says Radaj. Cool colors and earth tones are good, reds and yellows, not so much.

Edit the toy chest. For a dog's toys, use a low box or basket he can get into himself and edit toys to a few good ones at a time, weeding out those your dog doesn't play with and rotating the selection.

Create an escape room. In a far corner of a guest room or den—or under a piece of furniture—create a place where your dog can go to get away from it all.

THE WELL-APPOINTED DOG HOME

You didn't think you could just throw an old pillow in the corner and consider your house canine ready, did you? No modern dog home is complete without the following accessories:

Audio speakers designed for dogs. My Pet Speaker is designed for your dog's delicate hearing and conveys higher- and lower-frequency sounds audible only to pets.

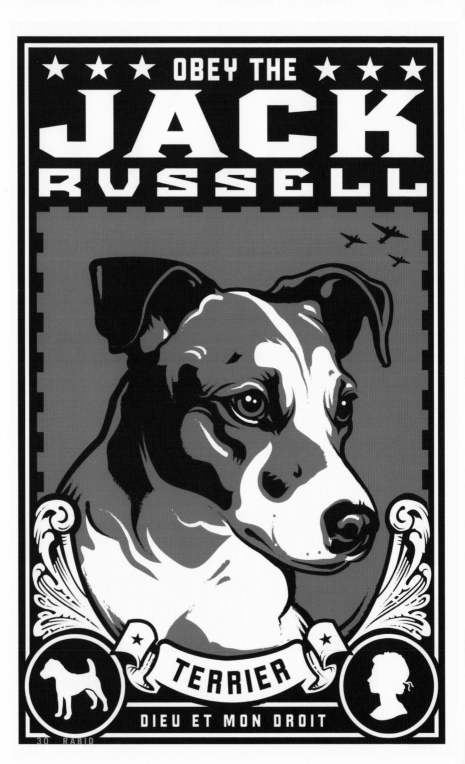

Aromatherapy candles. Specially made for homes with dogs, these aromatherapy candles promise not only to deodorize but to improve whatever it is that's ailing your dog in the first place. One scent that might prove useful: Fart & Away.

A bone-shaped fleece cushion. Is it a travel pillow? A teeny tiny dog bed? No matter, now your dog won't have to share your pillow.

Padded step stool. For the short-legged dog, stairs in soft fleece help her climb up into your bed or onto the sofa, and if she falls, she won't get hurt.

Folding gate. Like child gates but made especially for dogs, this will keep your pet corralled in her corner of the house—or you corralled in yours.

Dog-friendly videos. If you need something to keep your dog busy while you cook his night stew or iron her party dress, invest in a video aimed specifically at dogs, featuring raccoons, squirrels, mice, cats, and other dogs, with eight levels of sound including some audible only to your pooch.

Doggie dictator poster. You know your dog is in absolute charge of everything, so why not acknowledge her supremacy to the world with a brightly colored Mao-style poster extolling her breed.

Faux-fur pet pocket. Think of it as a sleeping bag for your dog.

Going to the Dogs

Traveling has become a whole new adventure, whether you're doing it with your dogs or they're going on vacation all by themselves. Among the dog hotel and resort options:

DOG RESORTS

Judging from a few roadside joints we've seen, many an old-school country kennel has taken to calling itself a luxury pet resort. But a scruffy dog run and some rickety cages don't cut it anymore. True luxury pet resorts today feature private suites with real beds, spa services, televisions airing dog-friendly fare, and private phone calls from owners.

Disney World, for instance, has a new Best Friends Pet Care resort where dogs can join a playgroup or have bedtime stories read to them.

Other top-of-the-line dog resorts offer such amenities as outdoor massages (with the therapist "speaking softly" to your dog throughout), canine hydrotherapy, acupuncture, online photos so you can keep track of how your dog is doing during his stay, and even a kiss goodnight.

PEOPLE RESORTS WITH DOG ACCOMMODATIONS

One Bal Harbour Resort & Spa is a luxury resort for humans that welcomes dogs, offering special dog beds, a chef-created canine menu, and bottled water for pets.

Kimpton is a midpriced hotel chain that offers a HosPETality program, which includes gourmet pet treats, dog walking, and pet massage.

CRAZY about your dog

Wanting your dog to live inside with you instead of staying out in the heat or cold.

▶

Buying your dog a cozy bed of her own but letting her sleep on your bed instead.

▶

Choosing a dog-friendly vacation rental for your summer week at the beach.

▶

Just CRAZY

Building an elaborate doghouse and then never making your dog stay in it.

Letting her sleep on your bed, under the covers, with her head on the pillow, right beside yours.

Turning down a free week in London because their crazy—crazy!—animal quarantine policies won't allow you to bring your dog along.

DOG
FOOD

Not the Same Old Dog Food

Dog food, like people food, has undergone a revolution—or rather, also like people food, several sometimes conflicting and confusing revolutions.

There's the homemade dog-food movement, for instance, which can mean anything from creating your own kibble from some combination of protein, carbohydrates, vitamins, and minerals to home cooking everything from dinner stews to breakfast muffins for your pet.

Then there's the raw food movement, sometimes called BARF—which stands for either "bones and raw foods" or "biologically appropriate raw food," proponents disagree—which is also often homemade. One BARF website describes the following as a daily BARF diet for a golden retriever: 12 (raw) chicken necks, an egg or yogurt, three-quarters of a cup of pureed raw vegetables such as carrots, turnips, parsnips, and celery, a teaspoon of oil, plus vitamin and mineral supplements such as nutritional yeast and alfalfa powder. Twice a week, add some tripe or uncooked liver or heart.

Homemade and BARF diets are often (but not always) also organic, as are vegetarian or vegan dog diets, though while vegetarian and vegan dog food may be homemade, it's never BARF. While a vegetarian dog may eat eggs, dairy products, or even seafood such as canned mackerel, a vegan dog eats no animal products. A vegan diet for canines might include—besides vegetables—rice, lentils, soy milk, and spaghetti with tomato sauce, which dogs reportedly love.

Gourmet dog-food purveyors—high-end butchers and name-brand chefs—are trying to address the tastes of all of the above, especially since most kinds of alternative dog food cost up to ten times as much as Lassie-era kibble.

Other companies are marketing food aimed to certain breeds or life phases such as puppies or elderly dogs. This may be as simple as small-bite foods to accommodate Chihuahuas or as complex as "food native to cold climates" for Siberian huskies—which is kind of like saying that everybody whose ancestors came from Scandinavia should eat only lutefisk and lingonberries.

The rationale, real or imagined, behind many of these new diet trends is health. Canned dog food has a long history of unsavoriness, dating back to its invention in the 1930s as a use for horsemeat and continuing today with ingredients that are leftovers deemed unfit for human consumption: "heads, feet, bones, blood, intestines, lungs, spleens, livers, ligaments, fat trimming, unborn babies," according to one website.

Detractors of conventional dog food blame it for maladies ranging from low energy to dull coat, osteoporosis to canine cancer. And it's a fact that pet food is recalled more often than human food: production standards are generally lower and food is more prone to bacterial infestation.

Still, many dogs become ill during the transition from conventional food to any alternative diet: vomiting, suffering from diarrhea, refusing food. Many vets discourage home-concocted or vegan diets as not giving dogs the nutrients they need. And feeding your pet "therapeutic" kangaroo meat purported to "enhance his immune system" is likely to produce results that are iffy at best.

COMMERCIAL DOG FOOD IS GARBAGE, PROPONENTS OF ALTERNATIVE DIETS SAY, THOUGH A HUNGRY DOG MAY NOT CARE.

YOU DON'T HAVE TO
BE HUMAN TO LOVE
CUPCAKES.

DOG TREATS

While dog food has become as serious as turtle meat and vegan patties, the dog-treat market has exploded in whimsical variety—possibly to make Fido feel better about having to eat all those carrots. Choices include:

- Bull-penis chew toys

- Chicken-flavored doggie bagels

- Frosting-drizzled donuts with sesame seed sprinkles

- Rawhide waffles with baked-in syrup

- Celery-flavored dog treats (Note: don't be surprised if, at the end of the party, most of these are still left in the bowl.)

- Nathan's hot dog treats

- Newman's Own organic cheese treats

- Bacon-flavored microwaveable popcorn

- Pizza with real mozzarella and pepperoni

- Carob-tailed squirrel-shaped biscuits

- Hypoallergenic cookies: no wheat, corn, soy, or gluten

- Red-velvet cupcakes with cream cheese icing

- Foie gras–flavored ice cream

- Mini cinnamon Bundt cakes

AND TO DRINK?

Bottled water or tap? In today's dog-beverage world, that question holds, uh, water. Some of the selection on tap:

Toilet water. The K9 Water Co. offers bottled water in flavors like Toilet Water, Puddle Water, Hose Water, and Gutter Water. (Yes, seriously.)

Sports water. A company called dogdration is marketing electrolyte-replenishing sports water for dogs, also containing such additives as "ginseng for health."

Vitamin-enhanced drink. Sold in a can, like soda or beer, a drink called Petrol is a "dog treat beverage" that's made from purified water, vitamins, and "natural flavoring."

Puppuccino. While this is sold in a barista-style cup, its "pure and healthy" ingredients are "gently dehydrated"; i.e., it's not a drink but food.

Breath-freshening beverage. The Pet Beverage is a liquid food and water additive that purports to freshen breath and other pet odors by doing something—we really don't want to know what—to the animal's digestive system.

Varietal wines. Nonalcoholic and designed to be poured over food or lapped out of specially dog-modified goblets, these are guaranteed to give new meaning to the term "hit the sauce."

Bowser Beer. Nonalcoholic and noncarbonated, this dog-friendly beer is made from beef and malt barley and now contains glucosamine because that makes dog owners feel virtuous instead of just cheesy.

The hard stuff. Johnnie Barker Black Lab-el looks like the scotch, but to your dog, tastes more like liquefied turkey byproducts. But the pooch hooch is off the shelves after the makers of the original liquor sued for trademark infringement.

HALLOWEEN DOG SMOOTHIE

Because sewing that Princess Leia costume for your beagle just wasn't enough.

1 cup kefir—low-fat, plain organic is best
A few oz. organic, unseasoned chicken stock
A nice slice of cooked liver
¼ lightly steamed organic (large) carrot
A dollop of canned pumpkin (make sure it's pure pumpkin, k?)
A splash of apple juice
A few slices of banana
1 tsp. of flaxseed
Small spinach leaf

HOW TO MAKE IT:

Throw all the ingredients into a blender (except the flaxseed and spinach leaf, add those after) and mix well. Serve immediately in a stainless steel dish, or chill for an hour in the fridge for a cooler treat. Sprinkle with crushed flaxseed and small spinach leaf.

Courtesy of raiseagreendog.com.

DOG-FOOD ACCESSORIES

Now that you have all that great new dog food, you can't just serve it in a plain old dog dish, can you? Why not look into some fancier canine tableware.

- **Talking dog-food bowl.** Imagine the sound of your voice coaching your dog through his meal: "Good boy, clean your plate, you're such a good eater . . ."

- **Raised bowl.** Why should your dog eat from an ordinary bowl when he can eat from a raised replica of a medieval goblet?

- **Dishes embedded in reclaimed wood.** High design meets green consciousness.

- **Dog placemats.** Because yesterday's newspaper just won't do.

- **Wine glass and plates.** So your dog can eat at the table with you.

- **Interactive feeder.** Your dog has to turn wheels or open sliding doors to get the food, which is fun, challenging, and makes him eat more slowly.

- **The Membo.** Kind of like a pill minder for dog food, so you don't feed Fido twice or not at all.

- **Drinking fountain.** Sleekly designed water fountain that encourages dogs to drink more.

- **Dog-treat launcher.** Why stop at delicious when you can have fun and delicious?

THE PUDGY PUPPY

All this good eating has created a doggie weight problem, with one study claiming more than half of dogs are overweight or obese. And it's all our fault says the top expert in the field.

"Legions of dogs are trained that every time they go outside and fake a potty movement, they come back in and get food," says Dr. Ernie Ward, founder and president of the Association for Pet Obesity Prevention and author of *Chow Hounds: Why Our Dogs Are Getting Fatter.* "It's dessert for breakfast, lunch, and dinner for our pets."

Letting your dog get fat can have negative consequences for more than just his health: one couple was convicted of animal cruelty for letting their Lab balloon to twice his normal weight, which made it difficult for him to stand up and caused breathing problems.

So how do your battle your dog's bulge? The only thing that works, according to Dr. Ward, is the same kind of regimen that feels all too familiar from our own weight struggles: higher-protein, lower-fat, lower-carb food combined with more exercise. But don't expect your dog to like going on a diet any more than you do.

"When you start cutting the calories, dogs crave sugary starchy foods and they're going to start begging."

If desperate, you might want to resort to one of these new doggie weight-loss products.

- **Doggie diet pill—Slentrol by Pfizer**

- **Low-carb dog food and treats**

- **Low-fat pig-ear dog chews**

- **Feeder that automates portion control**

- **Dog treadmills and treadwheels**

CRAZY? Fat Camp for Dogs

Several pet resorts and care centers around the country are advertising fat camps (yup, they're calling them that) for dogs, with a low-calorie food regimen, plenty of exercise, and even fitness challenges to crown the Biggest (Weight) Losers, both dog and owner.

SSSSSH. DON'T TELL HIM IT'S NOT A BONE.

DOGS *AS* FOOD

Dog has been eaten as emergency food in many areas of the world throughout history, but today its consumption is largely confined to a handful of Asian countries with strong dog-eating traditions.

Dogmeat is a delicacy that's often on the party menu in North Vietnam, where restaurants specializing in barbecued dog are especially popular at the end of each lunar month when dining on dog is believed to purge bad luck.

In Korea, where one in three people have reportedly eaten dogmeat, 2 million dogs are still eaten every year. Eating dogs is believed to increase energy and virility. But only mutts are on the menu: people balk at the idea of consuming purebred pups.

Called "fragrant meat" in China, dog eating dates back thousands of years and has long been popular in winter months as dogmeat was thought to increase body warmth. But as the popularity of dogs as pets increases in China, there's a growing outcry against dogs as dinner.

Protesters put a stop to a six-hundred-year-old dog-eating festival in China last year. Fifteen thousand dogs had been slaughtered annually for the feast in Qianxi, commemorating a battle fought in the town, but the feast was recently banned after a social media outcry.

And while dog stealing has long been a danger in countries where dogs are eaten—an average-size animal can sell for $100, which can easily equal a monthly salary—animal rights vigilantes have in recent years foiled dognappers and set trapped animals free. In China last year, two hundred dog lovers waylaid a truck containing more than five hundred dogs en route to the meat factory and paid off the driver $17,000 to release the animals.

The rescued dogs were then taken to a local animal shelter, where they lived happily ever after. Or something.

CRAZY about your dog

Traveling ten miles to the grocery store that stocks the canned duck liver your dog adores.

> Hand grating carrots to bake the vegan muffin treats you wish your dog adored—but that you end up eating yourself.

Using expensive-but-delicious gourmet treats to train your pet.

> Plying him with so many expensive-but-delicious gourmet treats that you then need to put him on a diet.

Taking up running with your dog to help you both lose weight.

> Buying a treadmill so he can run on it while you watch the football game.

Just CRAZY

SICK
PUPPY

The Well Dog

Pet owners spend more than $13 billion a year on veterinary bills, with dog owners averaging $655 a year in vet bills, up 47 percent in the past decade, according to the American Pet Products Association.

While regular vet visits are down for dogs, more dog owners are buying health insurance, which costs anywhere from $5 to more than $75 a month.

Some of the increased expense is for preventative care procedures and treatments not available until recently. These include:

Dog flu shots. While dog flu was only first reported in 2004, there's already a shot for that, at $35.

Melanoma vaccine. Lucky dogs. There are virtually no cancer vaccines for people, but the therapeutic drug Oncept helps prevent melanoma in dogs, who contract it the same way people do, from sun exposure.

Stem cell therapy. Ethics laws give dogs another advantage with stem cell therapy, being used on canines to treat arthritis.

Personalized medicine. Treatment based on your dog's individual genetic profile may not be here yet, but it will be within the next twenty years, theorized one doctor. The Georgie Project at the University of Utah is working on canine genetic disease mapping.

Birth control. Chemspay for female dogs is still a decade from production, while male dog birth control Neutersol was approved in 2005 but is not available in the United States because of a manufacturing dispute.

Laser surgery. It's a little more expensive, but lasers simplify such routine surgeries as spaying, neutering, and declawing for dogs.

Paternity testing. A UK service is about to start offering paternity testing for dogs, along with other DNA tests for diseases and breeding.

Prosthetics. Vets are working on advanced prosthetic legs for dogs and are also developing implants that fuse metal rods to the animal's own bones and attach them to an artificial paw.

Blood donors. An online service lets you register your pet to be a donor or to seek a blood donation.

Multivitamins. There are canine vitamins on the market for everything from joint pain to memory to anxiety. They sell well, but do they work? As conclusively as they do for humans.

TEN CRAZY THINGS TO KEEP IN YOUR DOG'S MEDICINE CABINET

1. Dog breath spray.
2. Peanut butter–flavored toothpaste.
3. Hot pants, for the dog in heat.
4. Pills that make your dog stop eating poop. How do they work? Who cares, as long as they do.
5. Master blaster high-speed dog hair dryer.
6. Dog Appeasing Pheromone (DAP) spray or plug-in that mimics the pheromone produced by a nursing mother dog and eases separation anxiety.
7. Disposable pet wipes—different types for eyes, ears, nose, paws, body.
8. Stop-snoring oral spray.
9. Anxiety-calming body wrap.
10. Patches that claim to enhance energy, ease dementia, aid detox.

CRAZY? Patch the Pot-Loving Pup

Medical marijuana for dogs? Yes, and they don't have to smoke the stuff either. A Seattle company called Medical Marijuana Delivery Systems is marketing a pot patch for pups. The only catch is that your dog can't qualify as a patient under the law, so you'll have to apply to state licensing authorities for certification—and yeah, you and your dog can share the stuff.

ALTERNATIVE THERAPIES FOR DOGS

Conventional medical treatments may be new and improved and growing for dogs, but so are alternative therapies. Some options now available for pets:

Homeopathy. Homeopathy works in dogs the same way it does in humans: by administering remedies in highly concentrated form that taken at higher volume would cause the illness they aim to cure.

Chiropractic therapy. Dog chiropractors manipulate and adjust the animal's spine to ease muscle pains and skeletal misalignment, but also purport to open up "blocked energy flow."

Herbal teas. A company called the Honest Kitchen makes herbal teas especially for pets, preferable to giving your dog the same tea you brew for yourself, which may make him ill. Safer: use herbal tea as a doggie hair rinse.

Acupuncture and acupressure. Dog acupuncture and acupressure is said by some to have remarkable results on dogs in pain, dogs suffering from arthritis and other signs of aging, and may help a range of other health and emotional problems as well.

Massage. Canine massage developed in the 1990s and now is practiced by everyone from groomers to doggie resort workers to owners themselves. But more serious massage therapy can at least ease the symptoms of dog arthritis, a common problem, and most dogs love the attention.

Reiki. Reiki practitioners move their hands above the dog's body, sending healing energy vibrations to the animal. While such vibrations have not been scientifically shown to exist, reiki may relax your pet—though it's hard to imagine how dog reiki via phone, another option, could be beneficial.

Yoga. YogaDogz is a hilarious international phenomena produced by photographer Dan Borris—but it's mostly not real. Borris uses Photoshop to create his, well, downward dogs. And while there are yoga classes for dogs and their humans, by most reports the dogs don't like them very much.

Get the Condoms and the Squirt Gun, Stat

In an emergency, dog site pawnation.com recommends using common household items for doggie first aid. But do you know which household item works as which medical implement? See if you can match the item in column A to the function in column B.

Household Item	First Aid Function
1. Cookie sheet.	a. Put eye back in socket.
2. Canned pumpkin.	b. Work as a muzzle.
3. Condoms.	c. Soothe shock.
4. Hydrogen peroxide.	d. Perform acupuncture.
5. Karo syrup or honey.	e. Protect injured or bleeding paw.
6. K-Y Jelly.	f. Treat constipation *and* diarrhea.
7. Pliers.	g. Administer medicine.
8. Pantyhose.	h. Function as stretcher.
9. Safety pin.	i. Remove porcupine quills.
10. Squirt gun.	j. Prompt vomiting.

Key: 1, *h*; 2, *f*; 3, *e*; 4, *j*; 5, *c*; 6, *a*; 7, *i*; 8, *b*; 9, *d*; 10, *g*

CRAZY? Pooper Snoopers

An apartment complex is tracking down poop scoop scofflaws using DNA analysis of the evidence.

HUMAN-DOG
PSYCHOTHERAPY:
WHO'S THE
DOCTOR HERE?

DOG THERAPY

Dogs have received a lot of attention lately for their therapeutic prowess. From witness stands to cancer wards, kindergartens to law school libraries, therapeutic dogs are working to ease trauma and soothe stress for millions of humans.

Dogs have helped survivors of the 9/11 terrorist attacks and Hurricane Katrina recover, rape victims testify, and autistic children learn to read. They've provided comfort to patients facing terminal diagnoses and to wounded soldiers returning from the battlefield. Therapy dogs have been employed by such august institutions as Yale University, Memorial Sloan-Kettering Cancer Center, and the U.S. government.

TOP 10 REASONS YOUR DOG NEEDS A SHRINK

1. Forget the vegan patties. Forget the doggie donuts. All he wants is a fucking bone.
2. Those fake testicles? Not fooled.
3. Keeps imagining that frilly tutu is a bird attacking from behind.
4. Fifi is just not that into him.
5. Motorcycles. Noise, wheels, sparks: what else do you need to know?
6. The Sisyphean task of trying to deal with the eternal and endless tsunami of pee-mail.
7. That squirrel outside the window has obviously been sent from some faraway galaxy for the express purpose of driving him out of his mind.
8. You feed her twice a day. And you won't listen, no matter how often or how loudly she tries to tell you that she actually wants to eat eight times a day.
9. Can't help but take it personally that you consistently refuse to make it a threesome.
10. Wants to eat the baby but fears that could mean an end to pizza treats.

Of course, humans provide psychotherapy to dogs, too. Dog psychologists, many of them trainers who crave a fancier name, are called in to treat such disturbances as incessant barking, separation anxiety, or coprophagia. That's when a dog eats its own poop.

Psychologists who treat dogs differ from psychologists who treat humans in that they make house calls and rely on their canine patients' family members to describe the problem and carry out the cure—kind of like if your shrink asked your mom what she thought was wrong with you and then told her how to help you get better.

The dog patient gets to be in the room as the diagnosis is being made and the remedy dispensed, but until dogs learn to not only bark some facsimile of "I wuv you" but also to describe last night's disturbing daddy dream and verbalize the ambivalence of transference, dog psychotherapy will not resemble human psychotherapy so much as infant parenting advice.

"A dog's mind is pretty simple," says Dr. Gail Clark of Fort Collins, Colorado, who has a doctorate in psychology with a specialization in dog-human behavior and hangs out her virtual shingle at k9shrink.com. "Dogs don't have the game-playing humans have. Dogs are motivated by rewards and consequences. They want to be led. Dogs think in the now and that's the beauty of them."

Dr. Clark is always in the room with both her canine patient and its human family. She collects the history of the trouble and observes the interaction between the dog and its people, and then prescribes a course of action, solving most problems in a handful of sessions.

And to deal with really serious psychological issues, like facing a terminal illness or recovering from a criminal attack? For that, you're going to have to call in the dogs.

ARTIST SHEILA NORGATE'S INTERPRETATION OF FREUD AND HIS CANINE ASSISTANT THERAPISTS.

THERE'S A PILL FOR THAT

Phobias, depression, anxiety, irrational anger, having to sniff every third lamppost you pass—they're human psychiatric maladies, but they affect dogs, too. Dogs have a similar brain chemistry and limbic system as humans, so most human psychiatric drugs affect dogs in the same way.

Drug companies are developing canine versions of human psychopharmaceuticals—like a chewable, beef-flavored version of Prozac called Reconcile—and coming up with drugs developed especially for dogs, too.

Dog-specific phobias like cars and thunderstorms can be treated with Valium and Xanax, for instance, while canine separation anxiety can be addressed with a doggie drug called Clomicalm.

Critics say these problems are the result of poor training or trauma and that relying on drugs without dealing with the underlying emotional and behavioral problems is not an effective long-term solution. And there may be other nondrug but also nontraining solutions to emotional problems, such as tight body wraps for the 41 percent of dogs—according to Thundershirt, who have a stake in the figure—who suffer from anxiety.

But brain chemistry imbalances are as real in dogs as they are in humans. Drugs may help up to 60 percent of canine anxiety sufferers and 90 percent of those who are overly aggressive. But animal psychologists and trainers say medication needs to be augmented with behavioral modification techniques.

And what about that lamppost-sniffing issue? Yes, dogs get obsessive-compulsive disorders or OCD. As humans sometimes compulsively wash their hands, Labradors may suffer from something called "stump suck" in which they tongue their paws so often they lick off all the hair. Dogs may also chase their tails to the point of exhaustion or bark ceaselessly. The cause is often the same as in humans—low levels of serotonin—as is the medication used.

Just don't be tempted to share psychotropic drugs with your dog. You both need your own prescribing physicians and your own therapists or you could risk barking at squirrels while your dog starts questioning the meaning of life.

HOW TO BE A DOG PSYCHIC IN ELEVEN EASY STEPS

Wonder what kind of job you can do from home, for maybe like a hundred bucks an hour, that takes no education or training or special talent? Oh, and right, that doesn't require that you take off your clothes or give up your three-Ring-Ding-a-day habit? You got it: pet psychic!

1. Never call yourself a pet psychic. The preferred term is "animal communicator," which is kind of like solid-waste engineer or exotic dancer.

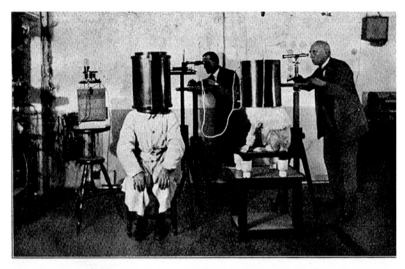

Abb. 21
Denkübertragung zwischen Mensch und Tier
Versuchsanordnung mit Klingelfuß'schen Hochfrequenzspulen
Zum evt. Nachweis einer Denk-„Strahlung"

2. Learn to recognize whether dogs look happy or sad, healthy or sick, friendly or angry, dead or alive. Or you know what? Don't bother. People are only going to pay money to have you communicate with dogs that are sad, sick, angry, or dead, and telling the difference between those is easier than cooking an order of fries.

3. Get your first customer. You can do this by appearing on television, building a website, advertising in media aimed at pet owners, or calling people who are looking for lost pets and saying you can tell them where their dog is—for a price.

4. Once you have an actual dog to communicate with, clear your mind. You know, like you do when your kids are talking or you're having sex.

5. Tune in to the visions, words, and feelings that pop into your head.

Everyone has this ability. You only have to know how to access it. Or at least that's what it says on the Internet.

6. Try to go national (or international!) and phone or Skype it in. That way you can make so much more money so much more easily and you won't have to actually touch the dog.

7. If using Skype, claim you can't work the video function. You don't want your customers to see *Jersey Shore* on mute in the background or that Ring Ding in your hand.

8. Okay, where were we? See, eight steps, already: this shit is *hard*!

9. Say what the dog is feeling, in dog voice. Dog voice, according to the most successful animal communicators, sounds kind of like the Indians sounded in pre–political correctness cartoons: Me no like can food. Me like people food! Old dog no smell good. Old dog smell sick. Me in happy place. Me be with Mommy again one day!

10. Remember you're selling hope where there has been despair, confidence where there has been desperation, certainty where there has been confusion. Keep your messages simple and positive, and don't get all hung up on truth.

11. Most important of all, get your money up front. And no refunds.

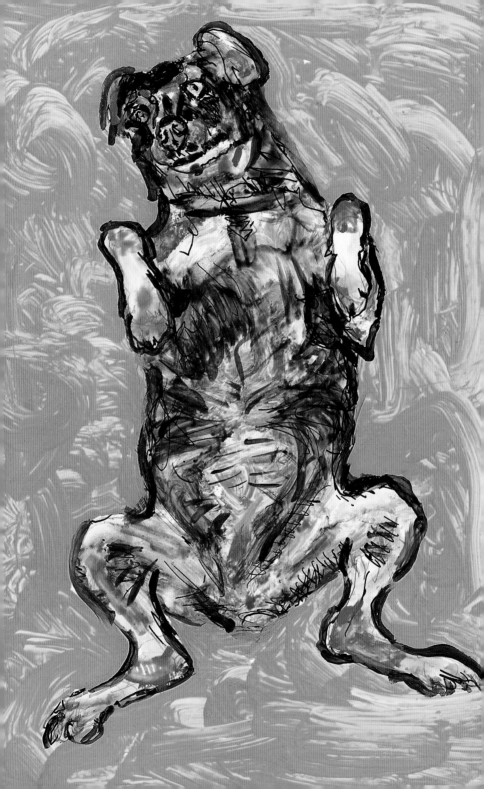

DOG HOROSCOPES

In case communicating psychically with your dog doesn't help, you may want to turn for illumination to dog astrology. One canine horoscope site, for instance, offers this: "The Aries Dog will never be a 'yes-dog.' The end relationship between the Aries Dog and his or her human will largely be one of compromise . . . usually on the part of the owner . . . but can be most enjoyable once the owner is 'trained.'"

Can dogs really be influenced by their daily horoscopes? Artist John Fleenor painted a series of dog portraits with the animals' daily horoscopes. You be the judge.

◀ ARIES. Romance rules the day as the Moon in your fourth house beams its light on new love. Self-esteem is at an all-time high for you.

▼ TAURUS. Financial matters will hold your attention for much of the day. Today's new moon in your eighth house of shared resources makes this a great time to meet with your financial adviser and go over your portfolio.

▶ GEMINI. With the moon in your area of status, you'll attract the notice of those in authority. If you're looking for work, today's new moon will give an amazing boost to your efforts.

◄ CANCER. This could be a major turning point when you decide whether to work through problems with your partner or go your separate ways. Could also be a good time to clean out closets!

▼ VIRGO. Your mind is stronger than usual and you yearn to connect with others in profound ways. Don't hold back: speaking the truth is the key to growth and transformation.

▼ LEO. Your ability to network will be at an all-time high as Jupiter moves through your house of connections. There are cosmic hints of behind-the-scenes events that could impact your public life.

► LIBRA. This is the perfect day to make travel plans. The month ahead could find you on distant shores for business, pleasure— or some delicious combination of the two.

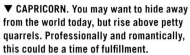

▼ CAPRICORN. You may want to hide away from the world today, but rise above petty quarrels. Professionally and romantically, this could be a time of fulfillment.

▲ SCORPIO. You might decide to make a change to your physical appearance or start a new project. If you truly desire to change your life, now is the time to make your move.

▼ AQUARIUS. What happens around the time of the new moon next week will bring together all of the efforts you have made since your last birthday. Your way with words and clear vision will impress those in power.

▲ SAGITTARIUS. This is a good time to shop for work clothes but don't go overboard on spending. This afternoon, laugh with friends and relax.

▲ PISCES. You may feel pressured to make an important business decision today. Changes brewing in your professional life require that you set up systems and schedules and stick to them.

CRAZY about your dog

Getting the peanut butter–flavored dog toothpaste so your dog doesn't freak out when you brush his teeth.

Treating your dog to a massage after an injury.

Consulting a dog psychologist.

Just CRAZY

Feeling guilty if you don't floss them.

Dog reiki. Really, really crazy: by phone.

Consulting a dog psychic.

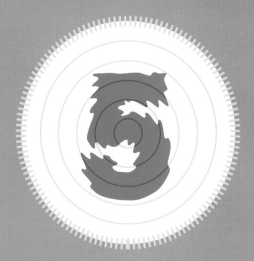

ARTS
AND
ENTERTAINMENT

Dogs and Art Timeline

Dogs have been important figures in all manner of art through the ages. A serious dog art timeline would have to include the following:

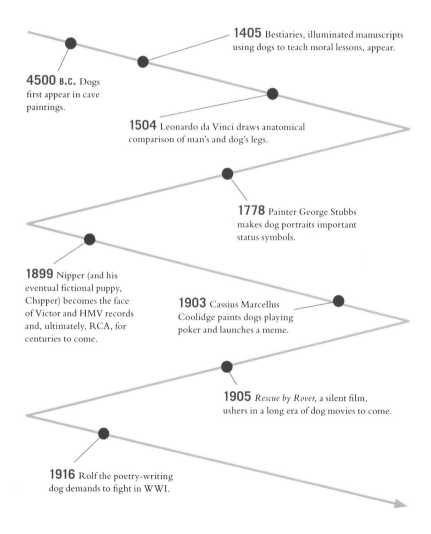

1405 Bestiaries, illuminated manuscripts using dogs to teach moral lessons, appear.

4500 B.C. Dogs first appear in cave paintings.

1504 Leonardo da Vinci draws anatomical comparison of man's and dog's legs.

1778 Painter George Stubbs makes dog portraits important status symbols.

1899 Nipper (and his eventual fictional puppy, Chipper) becomes the face of Victor and HMV records and, ultimately, RCA, for centuries to come.

1903 Cassius Marcellus Coolidge paints dogs playing poker and launches a meme.

1905 *Rescue by Rover*, a silent film, ushers in a long era of dog movies to come.

1916 Rolf the poetry-writing dog demands to fight in WWI.

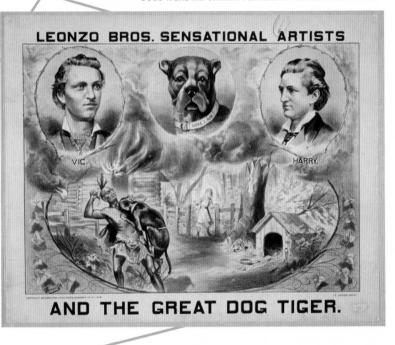

LEONZO BROS. SENSATIONAL ARTISTS

VIC.
HERE I AM
HARRY.

AND THE GREAT DOG TIGER.

1932 The original Rin Tin Tin, credited with saving Warner Brothers from bankruptcy, dies in Jean Harlow's arms.

1930 *The Dogway Melody*, a spoof on *The Broadway Melody* in which upright walking dogs sing, dance, and play all the roles, is released.

1950 World, meet Snoopy.

1939 Toto is paid $150 a week to star in *The Wizard of Oz*, three times as much as the Munchkins.

1956 Elvis Presley's "Hound Dog" tops the charts.

1954 Lassie, like so many stars of the era, had a gender secret: she was a he.

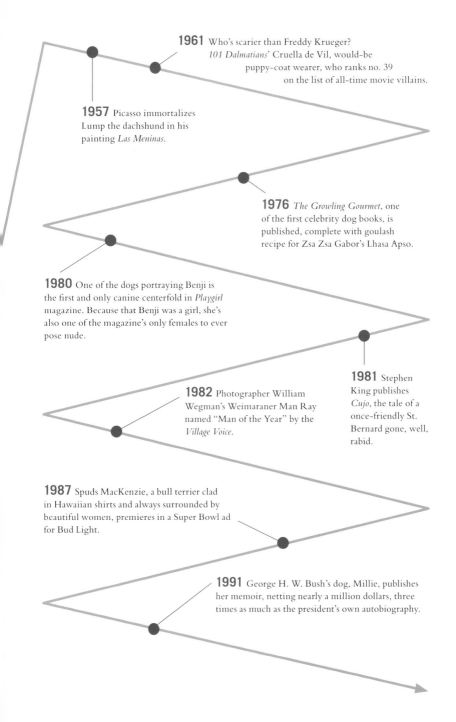

1961 Who's scarier than Freddy Krueger? *101 Dalmatians'* Cruella de Vil, would-be puppy-coat wearer, who ranks no. 39 on the list of all-time movie villains.

1957 Picasso immortalizes Lump the dachshund in his painting *Las Meninas.*

1976 *The Growling Gourmet*, one of the first celebrity dog books, is published, complete with goulash recipe for Zsa Zsa Gabor's Lhasa Apso.

1980 One of the dogs portraying Benji is the first and only canine centerfold in *Playgirl* magazine. Because that Benji was a girl, she's also one of the magazine's only females to ever pose nude.

1982 Photographer William Wegman's Weimaraner Man Ray named "Man of the Year" by the *Village Voice.*

1981 Stephen King publishes *Cujo*, the tale of a once-friendly St. Bernard gone, well, rabid.

1987 Spuds MacKenzie, a bull terrier clad in Hawaiian shirts and always surrounded by beautiful women, premieres in a Super Bowl ad for Bud Light.

1991 George H. W. Bush's dog, Millie, publishes her memoir, netting nearly a million dollars, three times as much as the president's own autobiography.

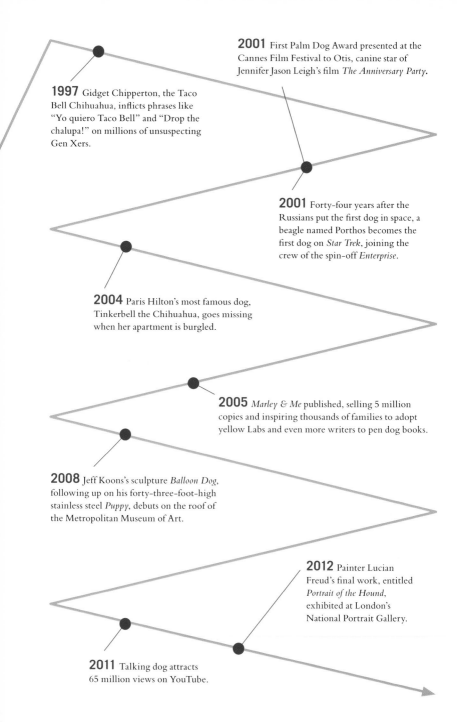

2001 First Palm Dog Award presented at the Cannes Film Festival to Otis, canine star of Jennifer Jason Leigh's film *The Anniversary Party*.

1997 Gidget Chipperton, the Taco Bell Chihuahua, inflicts phrases like "Yo quiero Taco Bell" and "Drop the chalupa!" on millions of unsuspecting Gen Xers.

2001 Forty-four years after the Russians put the first dog in space, a beagle named Porthos becomes the first dog on *Star Trek*, joining the crew of the spin-off *Enterprise*.

2004 Paris Hilton's most famous dog, Tinkerbell the Chihuahua, goes missing when her apartment is burgled.

2005 *Marley & Me* published, selling 5 million copies and inspiring thousands of families to adopt yellow Labs and even more writers to pen dog books.

2008 Jeff Koons's sculpture *Balloon Dog*, following up on his forty-three-foot-high stainless steel *Puppy*, debuts on the roof of the Metropolitan Museum of Art.

2012 Painter Lucian Freud's final work, entitled *Portrait of the Hound*, exhibited at London's National Portrait Gallery.

2011 Talking dog attracts 65 million views on YouTube.

Dogs and the Visual Arts

Dogs have been part of the visual arts as long as there's *been* art, appearing in cave paintings, in medieval tapestries, and in religious and mythological works.

Beyond the dog paintings, sculpture, and photographs that grace the halls (and in Jeff Koons's case, the rooftops) of high-end galleries

A DOG'S FACE IN THE MONA LISA IS THE HOTTEST SELLER OF DALLAS-BASED ART PAWS.

PAINTER JAMES KUHN
USES HIS OWN FACE
AS HIS CANVAS.

and museums, there's another flourishing world of dog art, in a range of forms. Thousands of painters, printmakers, and photographers specialize in dog portraits, for instance—attractive, often, but hardly remarkable. And then there are those visual artists who take things further:

Dog with Mona Lisa. Dallas artist Rebecca Collins runs Art Paws, which along with doing standard pet portraits will Photoshop your dog into a classic painting like *The Birth of Venus* or the *Mona Lisa*.

The dog goes round and round. Carousel carver Tim Racer fashions dogs into antique-style wooden carousel figures. His carved dogs are featured on carousels at the San Francisco Zoo and in Golden Gate Park.

The name makes the dog. Stephen Kline is a Florida artist who creates lithographs of dogs by writing the name of the breed—poodle, poodle, poodle—or your dog's individual name over and over and over. And over.

Dog face. James Kuhn's canvas is his own face, on which he paints entertaining and sometimes horrifying pictures of dogs and lots of other creatures—a new one every day. See more of him on Flickr at hawhawjames: he is amazing.

Let the dog paint his own damn picture. Tillamook Cheddar is "the world's preeminent canine artist," creating pictures with her nails that have been shown in galleries in New York and throughout Europe. If you wished your dog were more like Tillie, you might want to start her out with a Pup-casso interactive paint kit, which you can buy online for $20.

Dogs and Movies

Dogs have been popular stars, costars, and subjects of movies since the dawn of Hollywood.

TOP 10 BEST DOG MOVIES
Averaged from a range of Top 10 lists

1. *101 Dalmatians*
2. *Marley & Me*
3. *Old Yeller*
4. *Benji*
5. *Turner & Hooch*

6. *Lady and the Tramp*
7. *Lassie Come Home*
8. *Homeward Bound*
9. *Beethoven*
10. *Best in Show*

TOP 10 HIGHEST-GROSSING DOG MOVIES

If you are ever tempted to claim that *Scooby-Doo*, say, or the deathless classic *Beverly Hills Chihuahua* was a "stupid movie," I refer you to these earnings figures, in millions, according to Box Office Mojo. How much was it you said that you made?

1. *Scooby-Doo*	$153m
2. *Marley & Me*	$143m
3. *101 Dalmatians*	$136m
4. *Beverly Hills Chihuahua*	$94m
5. *Cats & Dogs*	$93m
6. *Scooby-Doo 2*	$84m
7. *Eight Below*	$81m
8. *Snow Dogs*	$81m
9. *Hotel for Dogs*	$73m
10. *Turner & Hooch*	$71m

Dogs and Television

From the earliest days of television, dog shows have been popular, but now we have Animal Planet, an entire channel devoted largely to dogs.

High-resolution television makes televised images look more realistic to dogs, who will respond to images of real dogs in motion—doggie videos featuring dogs and other animals moving—but not to cartoon dogs.

That's bad news for Goofy, though televised dogs come in all forms. Among the most popular canine shows and characters now and in the past:

VINTAGE

Lassie: The collie who always saved the day.

The Adventures of Rin Tin Tin: German Shepherd who was a hero of the Canadian Mounties.

The Littlest Hobo: Highly original concept—another hero Canadian German Shepherd.

KIDS' SHOWS

Blue's Clues: A man and his (blue) dog solve mysteries.

Scooby-Doo: A dog is the (very large) mascot of a mystery-solving team.

Wishbone: Talking dog acts out famous stories from literature.

FOR GROWN-UPS ONLY

Wilfred: A man hallucinates that his dog is a surly man in a dog suit.

Family Guy: Brian is a dog who walks upright, dates women, and went to Brown.

Inspector Rex: A German police drama about a crime dog.

ANIMAL PLANET

Bad Dog!: Bad dogs and very, very bad dogs.

Pit Bulls and Parolees: Pits and ex-cons rehabilitate each other.

It's Me or the Dog: Counselor helps couples and dogs achieve harmony.

Dogs and Music

There's music for dogs and then there's music about dogs. Each has its own, very individual appeal.

THE EMPEROR'S NEW SONG?

Remember when you were a kid and first learned that dogs could hear high-pitched sounds that we couldn't? That opened the door to the possibility of a whole secret dog world, where they were picking up high-frequency messages and communicating among themselves in ways we could never know.

Now a handful of musicians—and advertisers—have tapped into that secret world with music and other sounds that only dogs can hear.

On the high-art side, avant-garde musicians Lou Reed and Laurie Anderson put on a concert at Australia's Sydney Opera House that could be heard only by dogs.

In pop culture, a group called the Underdogs produced a Christmas single audible only to dogs as a fund-raiser for the SPCA. The title: "A Very Silent Night."

And at the purely commercial end of things, Nestlé ran a television dog-food commercial in Austria aimed directly at dogs, featuring sounds humans couldn't hear. Along the same lines, Nestlé created a sniffable dog poster. The idea is obviously that if pets respond excitedly to the commercials, their owners will buy the food.

But you have to wonder: exactly what sounds are they making to create that canine excitement? We're guessing it's less likely lip-smacking exclamations about how delicious the food is and more likely the chattering of squirrels in heat.

SONGS TO DANCE TO WITH YOUR DOG

"Call Me a Dog" by Hound Dog Taylor

"Puppy Love" by Lil' Bow Wow

"Puttin' on the Dog" by Tom Waits

"The Dog Is in the House" by Rude Dogs

"Who Let the Dogs Out (Barking Mad Mix)" by Baha Men

"Dog Days Are Over" by Florence and the Machine

"Doggystyle" by Snoop Dogg

CRAZY? Knit Your Own Dog

The crafts world has embraced dogs too, and one of the wackiest ideas—and most popular—is to knit your own dog. There's a website on the subject (knityourowndog.com/uk/), a book, and yes, even a couple of stop-action movies that picture hand-knit dogs wearing hand-knit sweaters playing with their hand-knit toys and never, best of all, dropping any dog poop, hand-knit or otherwise. The perfect pet (as the site says), indeed!

DOG BOOKS

There's an endless appetite for dog books, one that writers and publishers are only too eager to keep filling. (Imagine!) Some of the subjects new to the shelves:

- *Do Dogs Dream? Nearly Everything Your Dog Wants You to Know* by Stanley Coren
- *Reiki for Dogs* by Kathleen Prasad
- *The $60,000 Dog* by *New Yorker* writer Lauren Slater
- Several dog-related mysteries, including *Night of the Living Dogs* and *Fashion Faux Paw*
- Several war dog books, such as *Cry Havoc: The History of War Dogs* by Nigel Allsopp and *Canine Commandos* by Nigel Cawthorne, plus others by authors not named Nigel
- *How to Teach Relativity to Your Dog* by Chad Orzel
- Dogs speaking from the afterlife (doggie heaven is real!), with titles such as *Forever Faithful* and *I'm Home!*
- Books about pirate dogs, real and imaginary
- *A Jew's Best Friend?* by Rakefet Zalashik and Phillip Ackerman-Lieberman, about dogs and Jewish history
- *Dog-Friendly Gardening* by Karen Bush

- *Dangerous Book for Dogs: A Parody by Rex and Sparky*
- Rescue dogs who end up rescuing people, such as *Four Feet Tall and Rising* by Shorty Rossi
- *Dog, Inc.*, a book about the dog-cloning industry by John Woestendiek

SHE READ *RABID*, NOT TOTALLY AMUSED.

- *Chicken Soup for the Soul: I Can't Believe My Dog Did That!* by Jack Canfield, Mark Victor Hansen, and Jennifer Quasha
- *Dieting with My Dog* by Peggy Frezon
- *I Am Bill Gates' Dog*, a comic novel
- Books on dogs as a metaphor for success, such as *From Wags to Riches* and *Sales Dogs: You Do Not Have to Be an Attack Dog to Be Successful in Sales*, though none of them, as far as we know, by Bill Gates' dog

WHAT TO READ IF YOU'RE SICK OF DOG BOOKS

Is it any accident that many of the most successful works of literature of the past several years have the word dog in the title? They may not be dog books per se, but maybe it's enough that people think they are. Examples:

- *Black Dogs* by Ian McEwan
- *Don't Let's Go to the Dogs Tonight* by Alexandra Fuller
- *Isle of Dogs* by Patricia Cornwell
- *Started Early, Took My Dog* by Kate Atkinson
- *Love Is a Dog from Hell* by Charles Bukowski
- *Must Love Dogs* by Claire Cook
- *Road Dogs* by Elmore Leonard
- *The Curious Incident of the Dog in the Night-Time* by Mark Haddon
- *The Dogs of Babel* by Carolyn Parkhurst
- *The Dogs of War* by Frederick Forsyth
- *What the Dog Saw* by Malcolm Gladwell

DOG MAGAZINES

There are even more dog magazines in the United States than there are bridal or celebrity magazines, according to the titles available for subscription on Amazon. There are the big glossies like *Dog Fancy* and *Dog World*. Then there are the hip lifestyley magazines like *Bark*, *Modern Dog*, and *CityDog*. Alternative dog magazines include *Whole Dog Journal* and *Natural Dog*. There are even breed-specific titles such as *Pointing Dog Journal* and *Just Labs*. We can almost envision a magazine version of *Rabid* on the newsstand. (Psst, Si Newhouse, call us.)

FOURTEEN DOG WEBSITES TO WASTE A DAY ON

Believe us, we've been there . . .

Bad Dog Chronicles baddogs.com/: Where you can share your bad-dog stories, pictures, and videos and take pleasure in learning how much worse others have it.

Bee Dogs beedogs.com: "The premier online repository for pictures of dogs in bee costumes."

Celebrity Dog Watcher celebritydogwatcher.com/: If you're the kind of person who loves *Us Weekly*, but wishes it had more dogs, then this is the site for you.

Dachshund News dailydachshundanddognews.com/: Is there really that much to say about doxies? Uh, yeah.

Dog Central dogcentral.info/category/funny-dog-pictures/: Amazing, funny, and weird dog stories and pictures and more.

Dog Horoscopes doghoroscopes.com: Find out whether you and that puppy you're thinking of adopting are compatible.

Dog Quotations dogquotations.com/: A must-visit if you're heading to a doggie roast or wedding.

Dogbook www.facebook.com/Dogbookapp: Facebook for dogs, where 3.5 million dogs "interact daily" in a bark- and sniff-free virtual environment.

Doggelganger www.doggelganger.co.nz/: Want a dog that looks just like you? Doggelganger can help.

Dogs in Top Hats dogsintophats.tumblr.com: In the words of the site owner, "A different dog in a top hat every day, except when I'm too busy."

Dogster dogster.com: Cool and complete guide to dog ownership.

Hipster Puppies hipsterpuppies.tumblr.com: Dogs looking and thinking hipster.

I Has a Hotdog dogs.icanhascheezburger.com: U getz da meme?

Life With Dogs lifewithdogs.tv: The site for the person who watches only the dog videos on YouTube.

Wiki Fido wikifido.com: As thorough as a wiki can be.

DOG FESTIVALS

Thousands of Bark in the Park and dog-adoption festivals take place around the country and indeed the world every year. Some of the biggest and longest running:

UC Davis Picnic Day
Where: University of California at Davis
When: April
What: UC Davis is a school noted for its veterinary program, so it's no surprise that its annual open house, which has had a century-long run, features a number of dog-related events. The most famous is the Doxie Derby, a series of races for standard and miniature dachshunds. The dogs exhibit varying levels of seriousness; some don't seem to understand they're racing. Last year they added a "doxiecam" to one dog's head and broadcast it on the Jumbotron along with the scores. There's also a breed showcase and a Frisbee dog competition.
By the numbers: 50,000 total attendees at picnic day

Do Dah Day
Where: Rhodes and Caldwell Parks, Birmingham, Alabama
When: May
What: An annual parade and music festival that's been held for more than three decades now. The night before the festival, on Do Dah eve, the (human) kings and queens of Do Dah are crowned. The next day hundreds of pet owners parade on foot or via float with their dogs, cats, and exotic pets, followed by a free concert and complimentary food for both humans and animals. Attendees donate to local shelters and humane societies.
By the numbers: 45,000 humans and nearly that many dogs; $800,000 raised for charity since 1992

Bark Around the Park

Where: Millbrook Exchange Park in Raleigh, North Carolina

When: April

What: Organized by North Carolina Parks and Recreation, BAP is a dog festival started in the late 1980s that includes doggie Olympics with a sprint, high jump, hurdles, and a relay, a dog show, a Frisbee contest, bone hunts, and a booth to get your dog microchipped and/or vaccinated for rabies.

By the numbers: 3,500 attendees (human), $5 rabies shots, and $10 microchipping

Great North Dog Walk

Where: The Leas, South Shields, England

When: June

What: Guinness World Record holders for largest mass dog walk, which takes place along a three-and-a-half-mile route and also includes an all-day festival.

By the numbers: 22,742 dogs is the 2011 world record. They've raised a cumulative 4.2 million pounds over twenty years for charity.

Mighty Texas Dog Walk

Where: Austin, Texas

When: April

What: A fund-raiser for Texas hearing and service dogs, Mighty Texas has its eyes on the British world record. In 2011, they held the record for a few months, but the Brits got it back when they held the GNDW.

By the numbers: 11,256 dogs participated last year, raising over $250,000

Woofstock

Where: Sedgwick County Park in Wichita, Kansas

When: October

What: This Woofstock (there are at least three festivals that go by the same name), is an annual fund-raiser for the Kansas Humane Society that boasts events all day for dogs and people, including vendors, a silent auction, a play area for kids and puppies, races for all dogs, and competitions.

By the numbers: Average attendance 17,000; raised $200,000 in 2010

Doggie Art Festival

Where: Bullfish Baldwin Park in Winter Park, Florida

When: April

What: Exhibitions and sales by pet-inspired artists are the main draw at this festival, which also features pet product vendors and live music. Proceeds benefit greyhound rescue.

By the numbers: Thousands of attendees

Dog Bowl

Where: Fair Park, Texas

When: April

What: An annual free event at the Cotton Bowl football stadium, the park gates open to dogs of all shapes and sizes to run dog agility courses, perform dance exhibitions, have their pooch portraits painted, and play in giant dog pools. Meanwhile their people can visit vendors or adopt new puppies of their own.

By the numbers: Thousands of attendees

WAG! Fest

Where: Prairie Oak, Metro Parks, Columbus, Ohio

When: August

What: A festival that celebrates dog-human friendships and includes exhibitor booths and events including a Top Dog contest, which judges entrants on style, athleticism, and training as well as a dog-owner look-alike contest. Other features: a dog water park and disc and agility demonstrations.

By the numbers: 12,000 people and 7,000 dogs

National Dog Party Day

Where: New York City, San Francisco, and more

When: June 24

What: Pet expert Arden Moore and Pet Sitters International, the creators of Take Your Dog to Work Day, are trying to make June 24 an annual day of countrywide dog parties. Recent upscale events in New York City and San Francisco featured party games, fashion shows, and a flash mob, with plans to add more parties all around the country.

By the numbers: In its inaugural year, Dog Party Day raised $5,000 for charity.

Dog Halloween

Even if you're not the kind of person who might routinely outfit your dog in a Burberry jacket, say, and little rain boots, you may be tempted to buy or make him a costume for Halloween. While actual trick-or-treating could kill your canine—chocolate is toxic to dogs— you can always walk around the neighborhood scaring children or, more likely, scaring your actual dog.

The weight of a costume (or any kind of clothing) on a dog's back makes him feel as if he's being dominated and punished, says Alexandra Horowitz, who teaches canine cognition at Barnard, which can cause him to try to shed the costume by shaking it off, pawing it off, or rolling in a big pile of bird entrails so you're forced to throw the

damn thing in the garbage and let him stay home hiding his head in his paws whenever a trick-or-treater rings the doorbell.

"I haven't a (scientific) clue why people dress dogs up," e-mailed Horowitz, author of the book *Inside of a Dog: What Dogs See, Smell, and Know.*

Maybe because the pressure is on for you, too, with hundreds of doggie Halloween parades and festivals making you feel as if you, as a good dog parent, need to buy or make an ever-more-creative costume for your pet.

The trendiest right now:

Dogs as other animals. Bees are the most popular, followed by other insects such as butterflies and dragonflies. Other popular options are farm animals such as sheep or wild animals such as lions or dinosaurs. Cats are always funny; note that cat owners like to dress their pets up as dogs.

Dogs as famous people. Kate Middleton was big last Halloween. Sarah Palin is also a winner. And there are a lot of ways to go with Lady Gaga. For boy dogs, Elvis and Michael Jackson are stylish options.

Dogs as food. No. 1 idea: hotdogs, ha-ha. But tacos, bananas, ice cream sundaes, and the seasonally appropriate pumpkin are also big hits.

Dogs as food II. Attach a stuffed alligator or python to your dog's hind legs or an orca or shark to its head for that classic horror-movie look.

Dogs with riders on their backs. Knights, cowboys, Roman centurions, or even the Headless Horseman. This one is less of a costume and more of an action figure. But hey, it's easy and cute.

Star dogs. Some small dogs already look like Ewoks or like Chewbacca, so all you need is a hood or a belt. But Princess Leia and Yoda are popular dog costumes too.

Dogs as upright humans—with dog heads. There's a trend in store-bought costumes toward shirts with little stuffed arms, so from the front your dog looks like a little human with a big dog head. From the side, of course, your dog just looks like a dog with a tiny cloth torso hanging from its neck.

Dog-owner themed costumes. Nothing says "I love my dog" like making a tiny version of your own costume for your dog. Alternately, make your dog part of your costume and dress up as Dorothy and Toto, or Batman with a little doggie Robin.

Dog Sports

Dogs surfing in Malibu and skateboarding in Paris, kayaking in the Hamptons and disc-diving just about everywhere. Yeah, yeah, yeah: but what about the really over-the-top dog sports like:

Bikejoring. A cross between dog sledding and biking, with two harnessed dogs pulling bike and rider along wooded trails.

Canicross. Canicross is basically running while harnessed behind a dog. A fast dog. Like bikejoring, canicross originated to train and condition sled dogs in the off-season but has come into its own as a sport.

Dock diving. So-called dockdogs jump from docks for distance or height into a body of water. Popular around the world, dock diving is televised on ESPN.

Earthdog trials. These are a test of terriers' rat-catching ability, as teams of terriers navigate manmade tunnels on the scent of a rat (protected, lest you fear cruelty, by wooden bars).

Flyball. Flyball is a team relay sport in which four dogs take turns jumping hurdles and then land on a springboarded box that shoots a tennis ball into the air. Each dog then has to catch the ball (in its mouth, of course) and leap back over the hurdles to the starting line.

French ring sport. Originated as a test course for working dogs, they go through their usual paces: jumping, catching, heeling, guarding, attacking people dressed in protective clothing. Whee!

A DOCKDOG IN ACTION.

Hound trailing. Hounds race against one another on a ten-mile cross-country course, marked by an aniseed and paraffin scent.

Nose work. This sport grew out of training K9 rescue dogs. Also called scent work or fun nose work, dogs compete to match objects based only on scent.

Skijoring. Humans cross-country ski harnessed to a dog.

Tracking trial. People pretend to be lost, leaving objects along a trail and finally hiding themselves, and dogs track them via scent.

Treibball. In this new sport from Germany, dogs have to herd eight rubber balls, in order of color or size, into a net.

CRAZY about your dog

Tearing up at *Homeward Bound*.

Leaving the television on to keep your dog company.

Being a sucker for sappy dog books.

Just CRAZY

▸ Tearing up when Mishka the Talking Husky says, "I love you."

▸ Keeping track of your pet via doggie cam.

▸ Being a sucker for sappy dog commercials.

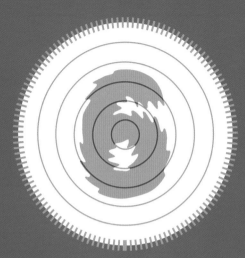

HOW MUCH
MUCH
IS THAT
DOGGIE?

Dogs and Money

Last year, Americans spent more than $50 billion on pets, half of that on supplies and vet care and another $20 million on food. The average dog owner spends about $750 a year on vet visits and vitamins, over $300 on food and treats, and nearly $400 on boarding and travel expenses.

Americans spend twice as much on pet products as they do on cosmetics, and nearly as much as they spend on toys. Three-quarters say they'd go into debt for their pets, and a fifth remember their dogs in their wills.

And animal spending is nearly recession-proof, with nearly 70 percent of dog owners saying the economy has no effect on their pet spending levels. At the highest end, not only are dog lovers willing to spend more, but there's also more to spend more on, including the dogs themselves.

THE WORLD'S MOST EXPENSIVE DOG PRODUCTS

How do rich people—or rich dogs—spend all that money? Here's how:

Snack: Four ounces of nonpasteurized red salmon caviar made especially for dogs, **$50**

Bowl: Puppy de Paris crystal dog bowl set in a gold frame, **$14,000**

Dress: Deni Alexander Golden Dream ball gown, **$3,000**

AT $3.2 MILLION, **THE MOST EXPENSIVE ITEM OF DOG JEWELRY IN THE WORLD, BY I LOVE DOGS DIAMONDS.**

Jewelry: The Amour Amour necklace from i Love Dogs Diamonds, which contains a 7 carat centerpiece diamond and 1,600 other diamonds hand-set in platinum and white gold on an alligator collar, **$3.2 million**

Carrier: Louis Vuitton monogrammed carrier, **$1,920**, or vintage Le Chien Birkin bag from Hermes, **$1,250**

Leash: Fluorescent calfskin dog leash from Balenciaga, **$295**

Bed: Royal Cabana linen and suede drapes and your pet's name written in Swarovski crystals, **$6,900**

Bathtub: Claw-footed tub with 46,928 hand-applied Swarovski crystals, **$5,500**

Perfume: Les Poochs brand VIP Dog perfume, four ounces for **$3,000**, or Sexy Beast unisex dog fragrance, **$850** including bottle engraved with your dog's name and hand numbered

DENI ALEXANDER DESIGNED THIS GOLDEN BALL GOWN, WHICH RETAILS FOR $3,000.

Nicole Geller

THE WORLD'S MOST EXPENSIVE DOGS

Sure, you can get a dog from the shelter or take on a rescue pup for a few hundred dollars or less, but then they wouldn't be able to . . .

Well, exactly what do expensive dogs offer that plain old mutts don't?

Status, for one thing.

The current "world's most expensive dog" is a rare red Tibetan mastiff bought by a Chinese coal baron for a million British pounds— nearly $2 million. The dog, named Big Splash, dines on chicken, beef, and abalone and is considered a bigger status symbol in China than cars or jewelry.

Tibetan mastiffs, sometimes called lion dogs, are believed to host the souls of nuns and monks who weren't good enough to be reincarnated as humans or to go to heaven. Genghis Khan reportedly numbered three hundred of the ancient breed among his army.

Other top-priced dogs may not have the spiritual or status advantages of the Tibetan mastiff, but carry other more practical qualities.

German shepherd guard dogs bred from special bloodlines by a company called Harrison K-9 Security Services in South Carolina have been sold to the U.S. Navy Seals, the British Special Forces— and a wealthy Minnesota couple who paid $230,000 for the dog's superior security instincts and skills.

The South Korean police own seven drug-sniffing dogs cloned at a cost of $100,000 each from an animal with a golden nose and then trained at a further $40,000 per dog.

The parents of a little girl with highly sensitive life-threatening food allergies paid $20,000 for a specially trained Portuguese water dog who goes everywhere with the child and can sniff out trace elements of dairy, eggs, and peanuts.

Where there's money, there's crime and black market deals.

In Iran, dogs have become high-fashion status symbols selling for up to $10,000 in under-the-table trading, despite or perhaps because of Islamic laws against dog ownership. Dogs are smuggled into the country and exchanged via wired money and blindfolded deliveries worthy of the international drug trade.

As the prices of dogs rise, dognappings are also on the increase, up 32 percent in the United States alone from 2010 to 2011. The stolen dogs, if purebred, are sold as pets or, if they don't have pedigree value, to research labs or dogfighting rings or, in Asia, to restaurants.

CRAZY? You Can't Be Too Rich, Too Thin, or Own Too Many Chihuahuas

A self-proclaimed dog hoarder in Mississippi bought seventy-five purebred dogs and then, after owning up to her problem, donated the animals to the local Humane Society. Would-be adopters lined up hours before opening time at the shelter to get one of the pedigreed animals for mutt prices. The producers of Animal Planet's *Confessions: Animal Hoarding* were believed to be seriously bummed.

THE WORLD'S RICHEST DOGS

If regular old people are spending more every year on their dogs, the economy be damned, rich people are going totally over the top.

Consider Britain's Louise Harris, for instance, who recently spent £20,000—that's nearly $40,000—on a wedding for her Yorkshire terrier, Lola, which included $1,000 for a wedding planner and $2,000 for flowers.

A Malaysian businessman spends more than $5,000 a month on his Tibetan mastiffs, which includes an air-conditioned enclosure and two full-time maids.

But while dogs owned by wealthy dog lovers and celebrities such as Oprah live pampered lives, the animals can become wealthy in their own right after their "parents" die. More than a million people in the United States have made their dogs the primary beneficiaries of their wills, which can mean big money. A self-published book by two attorneys called *Fat Cats and Lucky Dogs* advises pet owners on how to provide for their animals from beyond the grave.

Countess Carlotta Liebenstein of Germany left her Alsatian, Gunther III, $106 million when she died in 1992; his successor, Gunther IV, now claims to be the "wealthiest dog in the world" with a $300 million fortune. Gunther reportedly bought Madonna's Miami mansion and once bid $1,000 at auction on a rare white truffle, though Gunther's existence has recently been called into question—

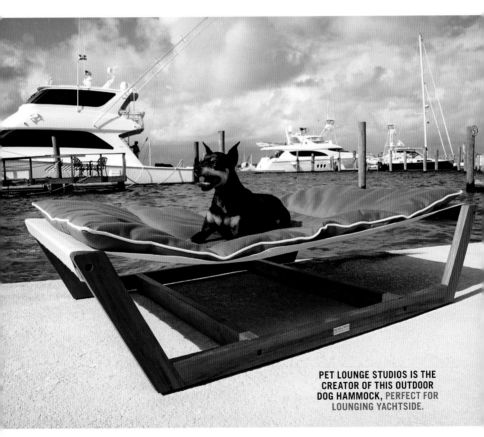

PET LOUNGE STUDIOS IS THE CREATOR OF THIS OUTDOOR DOG HAMMOCK, PERFECT FOR LOUNGING YACHTSIDE.

and really, his website looks pretty cheesy for a dog who's supposed to be that rich.

More easily verified is the $12 million bequest left by the Queen of Mean Leona Helmsley to her Maltese named Trouble, who was hand-fed by the housekeeper and encouraged by Helmsley to literally bite the hand that fed her. Although a judge later knocked the legacy down to $2 million, Trouble died last year in luxury at a Helmsley-owned hotel in Florida.

Heiress Gail Posner left a $3 million trust fund and her Miami mansion to her three dogs, one of whom wore a $15,000 diamond necklace by Cartier. Posner's only son contested the will. And back in 1931, another heiress, Ella Wendel, left her poodle Toby Rimes $80 million.

More recent dogs who inherited big from their famous owners include bull terriers Minter, Juice, and Callum, who received $82,000 in the will of fashion designer owner Alexander McQueen.

One of the largest private endowments is $300 million to Maddie's Fund, named for donors Dave and Cheryl Duffield's miniature schnauzer. The charity's mission is to save dog and cat lives; caviar dinners and diamond necklaces not necessary.

LUXURY SERVICES FOR DOGS

The pup who has everything can get used to being well taken care of, and there are service providers who are only too willing to accommodate—for a price. Among the services you can hire:

Dog stylist: Dara Foster, "fashionista in chief" of the site pupstyle.com and author of a book of the same name, will style your dog for red carpet events—or just lying around the house.

Personal trainer: Sure, you've heard of dog walkers, but Lindsay Stordahl is a dog runner, available to take your animal for a one-on-one run through the park at her Fargo, North Dakota, base. (So, yes, the upscale dog phenomena have penetrated even to North Dakota.)

Pet limo: A chauffeured car will drive your dog to the groomer, your country house, the airport.

Pet airways: That's right, the airport. This all-pet airways flies animals inside the cabin, with a vet onboard. Recent price for New York to L.A. roundtrip: $2,300.

Interview coach: Elena Gretch, founder of upmarket training service It's a Dog's Life, will prep your dog over the course of six sessions at $175 per for co-op board interviews.

CRAZY about your dog

Buying your dog a faux-fur coat—
if you live in Alaska.

▶ Letting your dog wear the diamond
necklace your husband gave you
for your birthday.

Choosing the car with the dog-
equipped rear compartment.

▶ Letting your dog ride shotgun, so
the two of you can really talk.

Making provisions in your will for
your dog's care.

▶ Dog: set for life. Kids: zero.

Just CRAZY

PUPPY
LOVE

The Social Dog

Almost all—92 percent—of dog owners see their dogs as members of the family. But for many pooch, uh, lovers, it goes much deeper than that. Nearly half of all dogs now sleep in the same bed as their owners, for example, up from a third a decade ago. And almost 40 percent of pet owners have more photos of their pets than of their significant others.

Whether your dog is your best friend or the love of your life, here are some new places and ways that dogs and their owners are interacting:

Dog happy hours and cocktail parties. In cities where dogs are allowed in bars, some establishments have started holding dog-friendly happy hours. At the One Bal Harbour hotel in Florida, mascot Lulu Flynn, "daughter" of entertaining expert Lara Shriftman, hosts cocktail parties for human-canine couples.

Dog-friendly restaurants. Not every place allows dogs in restaurants, but the venues—which include Florida, California, Minnesota, and most parts of Europe—are growing. The Dining Out Growth Act of 2011 allowing dogs to dine at outdoor restaurants passed last year in Maryland. Websites such as bringfido.com and dogfriendly.com list thousands of restaurants around the world that allow dogs. One restaurant in the UK even features a menu just for dogs.

Church socials. Churches have expanded occasional Blessings of the Animals to include dog-friendly church socials.

Social networking sites. Dogbook, Facebook's dog wing, allows dogs and their owners to connect on a wide scale, but locale-specific social networking sites have sprung up, too. Metropup.us is a Los Angeles networking site for dogs and their owners, for example, and thedogdish.com is centered in Oklahoma.

DOG MEET UPS

Everybody knows that walking your dog is a good way to meet other people. But in the age of the meet up, there are more organized ways for you and your dog to find your cohort, no matter how specialized that may be. Breedcentric groups abound and other sample meet ups include:

Brooklyn
- Supersocial small dogs
- Adopted dogs of NYC
- LGBT dog owners
- Holistic dog care and nutrition
- Yappy hour—wine lovers and their dogs
- Financial Fido—Wall St. workers and their dogs

San Francisco
- West San Francisco dog-friendly biography book group
- Muttville senior dog rescue
- Beaches and bonfires
- Berkeley Pomeranian lovers
- Bow-wow misfits

Chicago
- West Town pup crawl—outings to dog-friendly bars

Austin
- Metaphysical pets

Boston
- Snow dogs

Seattle
- Doga—yoga with your dog—group

DATING YOUR DOG

Can your dog help you find love? Three-quarters of women and half of men say they're more likely to date or marry someone who has a pet. And the new dogcentric dating websites such as AnimalAttraction .com or DateMyPet.com make it easier than hanging out in the dog park to meet the right dog owner.

Features that set these sites apart from regular dating sites are tools for setting up dog playdates, partner searches based on breed, and of-fline dog-owner events.

If it's your dog who's looking for the date, there's also an app for that. Mate Select UK Kennel Club helps breeders select mates for their dogs that will optimize the puppy offspring's health.

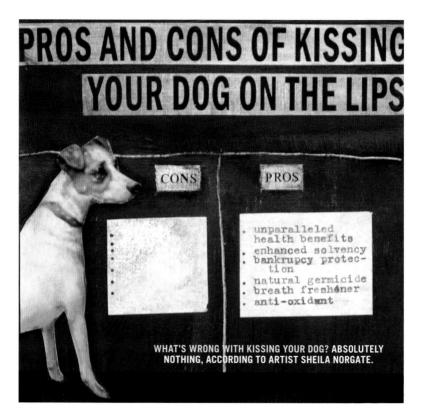

WHAT'S WRONG WITH KISSING YOUR DOG? ABSOLUTELY NOTHING, ACCORDING TO ARTIST SHEILA NORGATE.

TEST YOUR DOGGIE SEX IQ

WARNING: Exercise caution before reading. You can't unknow this stuff.

The family dog often provides a child's first lessons in sex education: "Mommy, why is Fluffy banging himself against the table leg like that?"

But beyond the basics, there's so much about dog sex we don't know—and believe me, may not wanna know.

Think you're ready? Think you've heard it all?

Okay, then. Take the following true or false quiz to test your knowledge on dogs and sex.

QUIZ

1. Two dogs in the same litter can have different fathers. **T   F**

2. There is a XXX-rated dog website called Zoo Tube. **T   F**

3. Is your dog lonely? There's a dog sex doll for that. **T   F**

4. Two men were arrested recently for using the Internet to find canine sex partners. **T   F**

5. You can buy a "massager" meant for dogs that's shaped like a bone.
   T   F

6. Meat-scented dog condoms were recalled as a choking hazard.
   T   F

7. Hector the Great Dane is a porn star in Hungary. **T   F**

8. In six years, one female dog can produce sixty-seven thousand descendants. **T   F**

9. An animal brothel in Washington State near the Canadian border attracted sex tourists from around the world until it was shut down by authorities in 2005. **T   F**

10. A woman died from an allergic reaction after having sex with an Alsatian. **T   F**

Key: All these statements are true.

CRAZY? Seriously, This Stuff's Hard to Get
Ten Great Dane puppies were recently born in Australia using sperm that a dog owner had kept frozen for twenty-one years.

DOG WEDDINGS

Dogs and weddings are two concepts that until recently didn't really go together. Now, though, of course they do, in a range of ways. You have your:

Dog-to-Dog Weddings

Once upon a time, like a whole half a decade ago, dog-to-dog weddings were Stupid Celebrity Pet Tricks, like the time Sacha Baron Cohen, a.k.a. Borat, charged out of the water to disrupt the wedding of Pamela Anderson's Chihuahua, Luca, to a golden retriever named Star. (And listen, we know what you're thinking, and we're not even going to go there.)

ONE HAPPY COUPLE.

Mini & Cooper just got Married

Today, though, you don't need to be Hollywood royalty to host a doggie wedding of your very own. Pet bridal finery, from veils to tuxes to ugly bridesmaids' dresses, is easily findable online, and a range of websites will instruct you on how to do everything from design the invitations to book a caterer.

In lieu of rings, for instance, you might dress the dogs in matching collars, and hosting the affair in an outdoor venue might make, ahem, cleanup after the guests easier. One site cautions that you make sure the wedding couple "get along," though as with other romantic trends sparked by Hollywood, monogamy may not be strictly required and quickie divorce is always an option.

People-to-People Weddings, with Dogs

Nearly 20 percent of dog owners want their pets involved in their weddings. One wedding planner, the Wedding Dog, even specializes

in weddings that involve canine friends and family of the happy couple.

Options? A doggie ring bearer's harness is available in custom fabric for $65 to $75, depending on size. Special training for your dog to walk down the aisle or sit still for the ceremony. And the wedding cake can even have a topper with your dog included, like the

STEAMPUNK WEDDING CAKE TOPPER BY ARTIST PETE POCHYLSKI OF BUILDERS STUDIO, WHICH SELLS FOR ABOUT $400.

Steampunk sculpture pictured here by Pete Pochylski of Builders Studio, which sells for about $400. (Note: you can get dogs-only wedding cake toppers too.)

Dog-to-People Weddings

Okay, these don't happen very often, and when they do, as with so many other awful events, they always seem to involve teeth.

One Indian boy, for instance, was married to a dog to protect him from animal spirits after a tooth grew out of his gum. Reports didn't mention whether orthodontia was first considered as a remedy.

And in Nepal, a seventy-five-year-old man married a dog because of a tradition that requires such nuptials if you regrow teeth after losing them. The man died three days later of unknown causes, though our best guess is that between the new set of teeth and the wedding night he might have been simply freaked out.

CRAZY about your dog	Just CRAZY
Making friends with other dog owners so that you and your dog can double date.	Insisting that your dog be included in every dinner invitation, every weekend in the country, everywhere you go, or you're not interested.
Using your dog as a wing, er, animal to aid in your quest to find true love.	Never finding anyone you love as much as your dog.
Dog makes a cameo appearance in the wedding photos.	Wedding takes place at the dog run.

DOGS
ARE THE
NEW KIDS

Parenting the Fur Baby

Have you ever heard someone compare their dogs to children? They're not just speaking metaphorically: more and more people consider their dogs to be kids, calling themselves parents and their dogs "fur babies."

In San Francisco, dogs now outnumber children, 150,000 to 108,000, according to the 2010 census. And in China, a recent governmental move to institute a one-dog policy similar to the one-child policy in effect for decades met with so much resistance that it was withdrawn.

How much are dogs really like children? Dogs have the developmental capacity of a two-year-old, according to some studies, and are capable of understanding something shy of two hundred words—though one psychologist reportedly taught his sheepdog to understand one thousand. New studies show that dogs share their owners' emotions and can "read their minds," mostly by being adept at interpreting physical and facial cues. For instance, according to one study, dogs won't beg from a person who's reading a book.

People tend to talk to their dogs in voices similar to those they use on their babies, with high-pitched tones, simple words, and present-tense verbs. With dogs, though, they tend to issue more orders, while with babies they will ask questions.

"Training a dog is not that different from the kind of guidance and nurturing and parenting you would give to a child," says Gail Clark, PhD, a dog psychologist and author of *Puppy Parenting.* "As a good parent you would have to be firm and loving at the same time, and that's parallel to what it means today to be a good parent to your dog."

Dogs vs. Kids

There may be a new TV show called *Puppies vs. Babies*, which is a cuteness contest, but what's the outcome of the real-life contest? How is owning a dog different from having a kid? And which is better, dogs or kids?

This chart will help you compare.

DOGS	ADVANTAGE	KIDS
Have to buy them.	→	In many cases can make them yourself, using equipment you probably have lying around the house.
Can choose breed, markings, gender, and size.	←	Pretty much have to take whatever you get.
Housebreaking.	→	Toilet training.
Favorite food: canned duck in "meaty juices."	=	Favorite food: frozen chicken nuggets with ketchup.
Chewed heel off favorite Prada pump.	=	Crayoned on favorite white silk blouse.
Spends day at pricey doggie day care.	→	Pricey day care can eventually morph into free public school.

DOGS	ADVANTAGE	KIDS
Licks your face.	→	Says, "You're the biggest, smartest, strongest, most beautiful person in the world."
Birthday? What's a birthday?	←	Demands expensive designer jeans for birthday.
Still licking your face.	←	Says, "You're the most horrible person on earth."
Boy, I'm glad that kid's finally gone so I have you all to myself again.	←	College tuition, apartment deposit, wedding costs.
Probably will kick off before you do.	→	Slight chance will take care of you in your old age.

FINAL TALLY: 5 for dogs, 4 for kids, 2 draws. WINNER: dogs!

DOGGIE DAY CARE

Sending your dog to day care rather than leaving him home all day alone got its start, according to one article, in San Francisco in the 1980s, but has only taken off in recent years with studies that say dogs suffer from separation anxiety and depression when left alone.

Getting your dog into the right doggie day care facility can be as high pressured as getting your child accepted at certain nursery schools, with interviews of both owner and dog. Typically, day care centers require that dogs have been vaccinated and spayed or neutered, and there are often size limits.

Prices range from $12 to $50 or so a day, with in-home care in smaller towns costing less than top-notch facilities in larger cities.

Most centers offer exercise, socialization, snacks, and naps, but some may include such amenities as on-site swimming pools, massages, and webcams so you can keep an eye on your dog when you're at work.

TAKE YOUR DOG TO WORK DAY

First came Take Our Daughters to Work Day, which morphed into Take Our Daughters and Sons to Work Day, and now we have Take Your Dog to Work Day, celebrated on June 24. In its thirteenth year, five thousand companies now participate in the event. Allowing dogs in the workplace, say the organizers, leads to more creativity and productivity, less absenteeism, and even longer hours.

HELICOPTER DOG PARENTING

What does it mean to be a good parent to your dog? Beyond enlightened care and training, conscious dog owners may invest in the following:

Digital dog activity monitor. If your dog is home without you rather than at doggie day care, this monitor tells you whether he's a couch potato—or tearing up the place.

Adventure Dog DVDs. These films promise to keep your pet not only entertained but "learning" even when you're not there.

Doggie and Me classes. You've heard of Mommy and Me? These are the same thing, but with fur babies.

Barking Boot Camp. Early morning boot camp exercise classes, with dogs.

DOGS HAVE
BEEN INTO
CELEBRATING
THEIR BIRTHDAYS
EVER SINCE
THEY FIGURED
OUT FOOD WAS
INVOLVED.

Dog birthday parties. Even if you're not crazy enough to marry off your dog, you might want to throw your pet a birthday party, complete with cute hats, animal friends, birthday cake, and a big wet birthday kiss.

DOG TOILET TRAINING

When I first read about dog toilet training, I was confused. *Really?* I thought. People are training dogs to use the actual toilet?

Well, yes, in a few cases. A YouTube video uploaded by someone named Poopeedog features a dog jumping up onto an actual toilet, peeing, then pooping, then blinking at the camera, no doubt thinking, *Seriously? You're filming me doing this?*

Or more to the point: Seriously? You're watching this? The answer is yes in nearly 150,000 cases, though the video offers no instructional content.

Usually, though, "toileting" refers to using one of the new pet "toilet" products, like the plastic trough that hooks into your plumbing system and features a handheld sprayer to wash away doggie waste, or one of those boxes that look like a putting green.

Disposable dog diapers are also available now, in tiny sizes for puppies or for older dogs.

And if you'd just like to train your dog the old-fashioned way, you can look for ecologically-sound waste bags that will biodegrade along with their contents.

NAME THAT DOGGIE

When your new neighbor calls for Max or Lola, do you think a child or a dog will come running? What about Buddy or Bear?

It's anyone's guess as more and more dogs get people names, while children are given dog names.

All the Top 10 names for both genders of dogs are human names now. Here, a recent popularity list:

Female	Male
Bella (Isabella was no. 1 for baby girls in 2010)	Max
	Charlie
Daisy	Jack
Molly	Buddy
Lucy	Jake (Jacob has for several years been the no. 1 name for baby boys)
Sadie	
Maggie	
Bailey	Tucker
Chloe	Duke
Sophie (Sophia was recently no. 2 for baby girls)	Toby
	Bear
Lola	Oscar

THIS DAD IS TAKING NO CHANCES WITH HIS FUR BABY.

Other popular people names also showing up for dogs include Lily, Zoe, and Ruby for girls and Cooper, Oliver, and Jasper for boys.

Buddy, Duke, and Bear are not people names, you say? Au contraire. Chef Jamie Oliver has a Buddy Bear while actress Alicia Silverstone's son is Bear. Justine Bateman and makeup mogul Bobbi Brown are both the mothers of boys named Duke.

EIGHTEEN THINGS EVERY FUR BABY DESERVES

Puppy- and dog-care products imitate baby and child products. Any diligent human parent will want to buy the following for her fur baby:

1. Puppy nursing bottle
2. Diapers (more, much more than you've ever wanted to know, on that later)
3. Chest carrier or carrying sling
4. New puppy binky
5. Puppy teething pacifier and ring
6. Teething gel
7. Bottle- and rattle-shaped toys
8. Squeak toys
9. Receiving blankets
10. Digital ear thermometer
11. Baby powder grooming spray
12. High chair
13. Dog stroller
14. Playpen
15. Car seat
16. Bike basket and trailer
17. Bike helmet
18. Doggie backpack (though there are also front packs in which to carry your pup)

Other celebrities whose children have canine-appropriate names include Mike Myers, whose son is Spike; Michele Hicks and Jonny Lee Miller, parents of Buster; Roseanne Barr, whose son is named Buck; Damon Dash, who has a son named Lucky; Gerard Way, who has a daughter named Bandit; and Robert Rodriguez, father of Rocket.

CRAZY? Breastfeeding Your Dog

A Ugandan man was arrested for forcing his wife to breastfeed his five puppies. His defense: he had no milk for them, having given his cows to his wife's family as a dowry.

TOY THINGS

Buster's gonna *scream* if you try to make him play with that nasty old tennis ball one more time. Dog toys have come a long way. Many of the most fascinating—for you and for your dog—fall into one of these categories:

Things you had when you were a kid. Rubber soldiers, say, or plastic dinosaurs, or dolls or wading pools, things that will bring back memories of your own childhood and that you might even play with when nobody (including Buster) is looking.

Things you'd have now, if you could afford them. Chanel bags or Cuban cigars. Champagne bottles or Tiffany boxes. Things you kinda want but couldn't possibly afford and so you make fun of them by buying cheap polyester fur versions for your dog.

Hipster so-uncool-they're-cool things. Stuffed cassette tapes, for instance, or orange peanuts like those marshmallow ones your grandmother used to try to make you eat.

Soothing things. A bone that smells like Mom and a pad that cools you down, they're cheaper than a doggie shrink and who knows, maybe just as effective. There's even a stuffed pillow called a Chill Pill.

Green things. Biodegradable, sustainable, and often locally made (check Etsy).

Techno things. Yeah, there's an app for that, like the squeaky app that emits a sound dogs seem to love.

Things designed to make your dog smarter. Puzzles and other interactive toys to challenge their little—okay, their growing, *totally growing!*—brains.

Things that are more fun for you than for your dog. A ball launcher. A ball that when he clutches it in his mouth makes him look like he's got a giant handlebar mustache. A scooter that you stand on while he pulls you along and you imagine you're competing in the Iditarod, though you just look like an idiot on a scooter being towed by your poor dog.

CRAZY about your dog		Just CRAZY
Calling your dog your "baby."	▶	Using your dog to try to bond over parenting experiences with your friend who just had an actual—yes, I mean human—baby.
Pulling strings to get dog into top-notch day care.	▶	Sleeping with someone to get dog into top-notch day care.
Angsting over the whole house-breaking thing.	▶	Dealing with it by putting up a fence and turning your yard into one big open-air dog toilet.

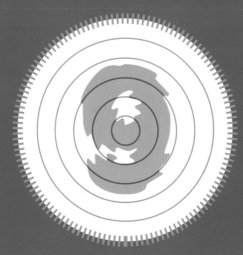

FAMOUS

DOGS

What's Your Celebrity-Dog IQ?

You know everything about their clothes, their love lives, their babies—and their dogs. Or do you? Test your celebrity-dog knowledge here.

QUIZ

1. Jennifer Aniston was so crazy about her dog, Norman, she did what when he died?

a. Cradled his stiff body in her arms and howled at the moon.

b. Had his ashes turned into a necklace.

c. Tattooed his name on her right foot.

2. Elton John's dog Arthur played what role at the singer's wedding?

a. Groom.

b. Minister.

c. Best man.

3. Mark Zuckerberg's dog Beast has over 350,000 what?

a. Dollars in the bank.

b. Pairs of Hipster Puppy sunglasses.

c. Likes on Dogbook.

4. Charlie Sheen's pug died of:

a. A drug overdose.

b. Embarrassment.

c. Malnutrition.

5. George and Laura Bush's terrier Barney did what to a journalist?

a. Used him like a lamppost.

b. Humped his leg like he meant it.

c. Bit him.

6. Lindsay Lohan paramour Samantha Ronson's bulldog did what to a Maltese in her Hollywood apartment building?

a. Married it.

b. Sold it out to the paparazzi.

c. Killed it.

7. Mariah Carey was sued for nonpayment by a vet who did what to the singer's prematurely born Jack Russell puppy?

a. Tube fed it.

b. Slept with it.

c. Tube fed it, slept with it, and videotaped the whole thing.

8. eBay bidders paid more than $300 for what item previously used by Paris Hilton's dog?

a. Little shiny doggie purse.

b. Little lacy doggie panties.

c. Empty smelly dog-food can.

9. A pooch previously owned by convicted dogfighter Michael Vick got what from the city of Dallas?

a. Front-row seats at the Cowboys' playoff game.

b. Tiny gold-plated boxing gloves.

c. An edible key to the city.

10. Because of a traumatic early experience, Marilyn Monroe refused to ever do what with a dog?

a. Pet one.

b. Date one.

c. Be photographed with one.

Key: The correct answer to every question is *c.*

CELEBRITY-DOG MATCHUP

Match the celebrity with his or her dog's name.

1. Marilyn Monroe	a. Sweetlips
2. Pete Wentz	b. Jazzmin
3. Jacqueline Kennedy	c. Blondie
4. George Washington	d. George
5. Audrey Hepburn	e. Audrey
6. Ozzy Osbourne	f. Ozzy
7. Brett Favre	g. Clipper
8. Oprah Winfrey	h. Famous
9. Adolf Hitler	i. Mafia
10. Rachael Ray	j. Dash
11. Queen Victoria	k. Boatswain
12. Ryan Gosling	l. Spike
13. Joan Rivers	m. Isaboo
14. Emily Brontë	n. Kola
15. Mila Kunis	o. Keeper
16. Dave Barry	p. Earnest
17. Lord Byron	q. Ernest Hemingway
18. Kellan Lutz	r. Sophie

Key: 1, *i*; 2, *q*; 3, *g*; 4, *a*; 5, *h*; 6, *f*; 7, *b*; 8, *r*; 9, *c*; 10, *m*; 11, *j*; 12, *d*; 13, *l*; 14, *o*; 15, *e*; 16, *p*; 17, *k*; 18, *n*

ROYAL DOGS TIMELINE

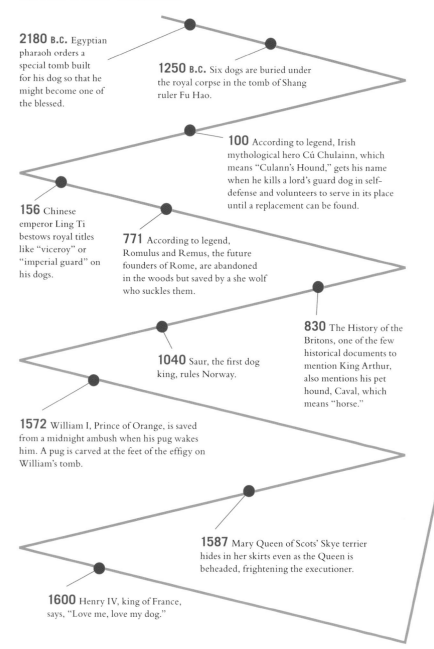

2180 B.C. Egyptian pharaoh orders a special tomb built for his dog so that he might become one of the blessed.

1250 B.C. Six dogs are buried under the royal corpse in the tomb of Shang ruler Fu Hao.

100 According to legend, Irish mythological hero Cú Chulainn, which means "Culann's Hound," gets his name when he kills a lord's guard dog in self-defense and volunteers to serve in its place until a replacement can be found.

156 Chinese emperor Ling Ti bestows royal titles like "viceroy" or "imperial guard" on his dogs.

771 According to legend, Romulus and Remus, the future founders of Rome, are abandoned in the woods but saved by a she wolf who suckles them.

830 The History of the Britons, one of the few historical documents to mention King Arthur, also mentions his pet hound, Caval, which means "horse."

1040 Saur, the first dog king, rules Norway.

1572 William I, Prince of Orange, is saved from a midnight ambush when his pug wakes him. A pug is carved at the feet of the effigy on William's tomb.

1587 Mary Queen of Scots' Skye terrier hides in her skirts even as the Queen is beheaded, frightening the executioner.

1600 Henry IV, king of France, says, "Love me, love my dog."

1640s Riding in front of his master, Prince Rupert, in the English Civil War, an oversized poodle named Boye becomes known as the devil dog of the cavaliers. He is thought to have supernatural powers, rendering his master impervious to harm.

1660s King Charles II issues a royal decree that Cavalier King Charles spaniels are to be allowed anywhere in England, including the Houses of Parliament.

1687 Under the reign of Tokugawa Tsunayoshi, "the dog shogun," over two thousand common people are put to death in a single year for harming dogs. In addition, several samurai are forced to commit seppuku for killing dogs.

1700s Toy poodles with elaborate haircuts are a popular fad in Louis XVI's royal court.

1796 As Napoleon Bonaparte makes love to his first wife, Josephine, on their wedding night, his bride's pet pug, Fortune, bites him on the calf, leading the general to a lifelong hatred of dogs.

1800 Princess of Prussia and Duchess of York Frederica Charlotte, Freddie to her friends, adores dogs and keeps as many as forty. Her husband, not so much: the royal couple separate, childless.

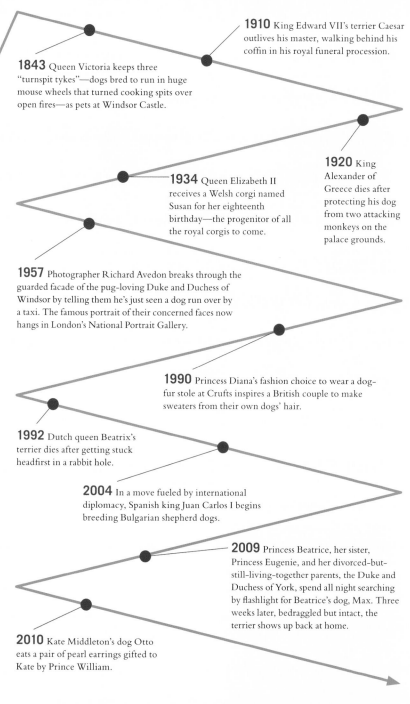

1843 Queen Victoria keeps three "turnspit tykes"—dogs bred to run in huge mouse wheels that turned cooking spits over open fires—as pets at Windsor Castle.

1910 King Edward VII's terrier Caesar outlives his master, walking behind his coffin in his royal funeral procession.

1934 Queen Elizabeth II receives a Welsh corgi named Susan for her eighteenth birthday—the progenitor of all the royal corgis to come.

1920 King Alexander of Greece dies after protecting his dog from two attacking monkeys on the palace grounds.

1957 Photographer Richard Avedon breaks through the guarded facade of the pug-loving Duke and Duchess of Windsor by telling them he's just seen a dog run over by a taxi. The famous portrait of their concerned faces now hangs in London's National Portrait Gallery.

1990 Princess Diana's fashion choice to wear a dog-fur stole at Crufts inspires a British couple to make sweaters from their own dogs' hair.

1992 Dutch queen Beatrix's terrier dies after getting stuck headfirst in a rabbit hole.

2004 In a move fueled by international diplomacy, Spanish king Juan Carlos I begins breeding Bulgarian shepherd dogs.

2009 Princess Beatrice, her sister, Princess Eugenie, and her divorced-but-still-living-together parents, the Duke and Duchess of York, spend all night searching by flashlight for Beatrice's dog, Max. Three weeks later, bedraggled but intact, the terrier shows up back at home.

2010 Kate Middleton's dog Otto eats a pair of pearl earrings gifted to Kate by Prince William.

CRAZY? Presidential Dog is a Lot of Work

Eighty volunteers spent five hundred hours fashioning a likeness of the Obamas' dog, Bo, as a White House Christmas decoration.

CRAZY about your dog	Just CRAZY
Following celebrity dog ownership as avidly as some people follow celebrity baby bumps.	Thinking that naming your dog Norman makes you soul sisters with Jennifer Aniston.
Judging a political candidate a little bit more positively if he has a dog.	Does he like dogs? He's got your vote.
Thinking your dog is more beautiful than Queen Elizabeth's corgis.	Thinking a corgi would have made a more beautiful bridesmaid than Pippa.

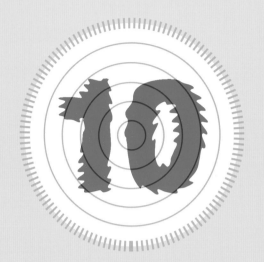

ARE DOGS
GOD?

The Evidence For and Against

Dogs have played important roles in many religions around the world from ancient times through the present. In Nepal, dogs are honored for their divine role once a year at the festival of Tihar, where dogs are festooned with flower garlands, given special food, and marked on their foreheads with a Tilak, the Hindu powder of blessing. In the Hindu religious epic Mahabharata, dogs travel to heaven and act as guards of the underworld.

DOGS AND RELIGION TIMELINE

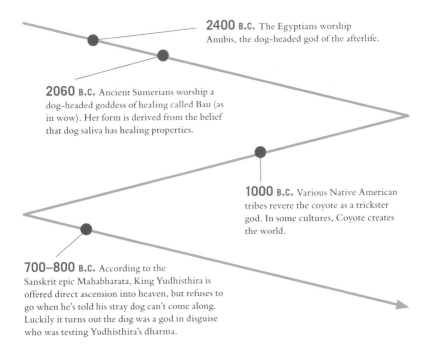

2400 B.C. The Egyptians worship Anubis, the dog-headed god of the afterlife.

2060 B.C. Ancient Sumerians worship a dog-headed goddess of healing called Bau (as in wow). Her form is derived from the belief that dog saliva has healing properties.

1000 B.C. Various Native American tribes revere the coyote as a trickster god. In some cultures, Coyote creates the world.

700–800 B.C. According to the Sanskrit epic Mahabharata, King Yudhisthira is offered direct ascension into heaven, but refuses to go when he's told his stray dog can't come along. Luckily it turns out the dog was a god in disguise who was testing Yudhisthira's dharma.

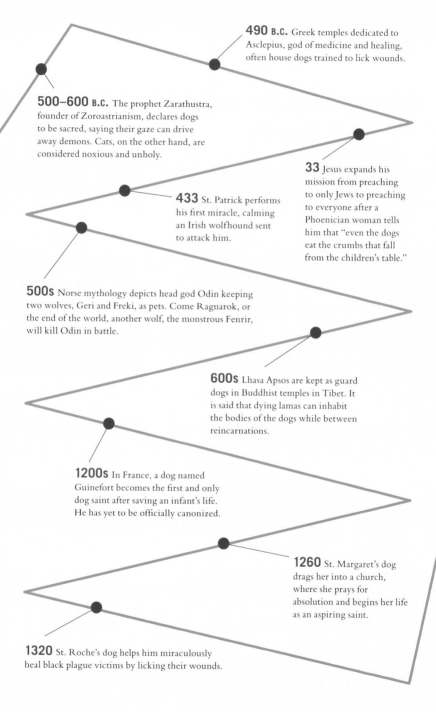

490 B.C. Greek temples dedicated to Asclepius, god of medicine and healing, often house dogs trained to lick wounds.

500–600 B.C. The prophet Zarathustra, founder of Zoroastrianism, declares dogs to be sacred, saying their gaze can drive away demons. Cats, on the other hand, are considered noxious and unholy.

433 St. Patrick performs his first miracle, calming an Irish wolfhound sent to attack him.

33 Jesus expands his mission from preaching to only Jews to preaching to everyone after a Phoenician woman tells him that "even the dogs eat the crumbs that fall from the children's table."

500s Norse mythology depicts head god Odin keeping two wolves, Geri and Freki, as pets. Come Ragnarok, or the end of the world, another wolf, the monstrous Fenrir, will kill Odin in battle.

600s Lhasa Apsos are kept as guard dogs in Buddhist temples in Tibet. It is said that dying lamas can inhabit the bodies of the dogs while between reincarnations.

1200s In France, a dog named Guinefort becomes the first and only dog saint after saving an infant's life. He has yet to be officially canonized.

1260 St. Margaret's dog drags her into a church, where she prays for absolution and begins her life as an aspiring saint.

1320 St. Roche's dog helps him miraculously heal black plague victims by licking their wounds.

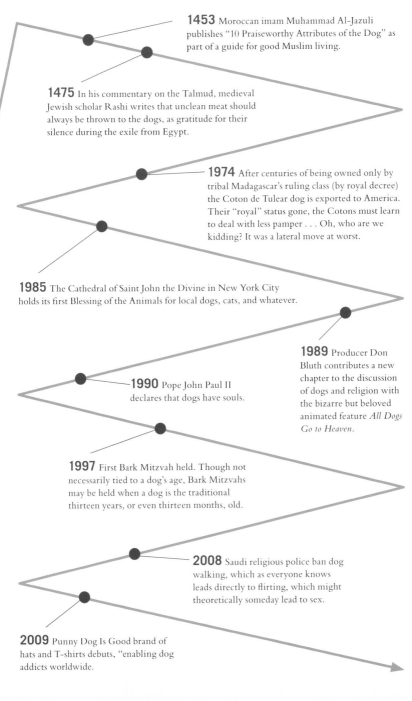

1453 Moroccan imam Muhammad Al-Jazuli publishes "10 Praiseworthy Attributes of the Dog" as part of a guide for good Muslim living.

1475 In his commentary on the Talmud, medieval Jewish scholar Rashi writes that unclean meat should always be thrown to the dogs, as gratitude for their silence during the exile from Egypt.

1974 After centuries of being owned only by tribal Madagascar's ruling class (by royal decree) the Coton de Tulear dog is exported to America. Their "royal" status gone, the Cotons must learn to deal with less pamper . . . Oh, who are we kidding? It was a lateral move at worst.

1985 The Cathedral of Saint John the Divine in New York City holds its first Blessing of the Animals for local dogs, cats, and whatever.

1989 Producer Don Bluth contributes a new chapter to the discussion of dogs and religion with the bizarre but beloved animated feature *All Dogs Go to Heaven.*

1990 Pope John Paul II declares that dogs have souls.

1997 First Bark Mitzvah held. Though not necessarily tied to a dog's age, Bark Mitzvahs may be held when a dog is the traditional thirteen years, or even thirteen months, old.

2008 Saudi religious police ban dog walking, which as everyone knows leads directly to flirting, which might theoretically someday lead to sex.

2009 Punny Dog Is Good brand of hats and T-shirts debuts, "enabling dog addicts worldwide.

DEVIL DOGS?

In ancient mythology, black dogs are often evil creatures, and things haven't improved much for black dogs today. Black dogs are seen as less friendly and more aggressive than dogs of other colors, and black dogs are more likely to end up in shelters and are slower to be adopted once they're there.

Nearly half—45 percent—of 120,000 shelter dogs in a 2011 study were black, more than twice the proportion of white dogs. The number of black dogs who are put to sleep is more than twice the number of brown dogs euthanized.

People have superstitions about black dogs that may not be as well known as those relating to cats but are every bit as negative. In folklore, black dogs are phantoms, haunt cemeteries and castles, and symbolize death. Black dogs are associated with electrical storms, executions, and depression. Some people believe black dogs are more aggressive and harder to train than those of other colors. And then there's the racist element.

Shelter workers even have a special name for the prejudice: black dog syndrome. To help black dogs get noticed and adopted, they may tie bright ribbons or bandannas around the dogs' necks or place brightly colored blankets or toys in their cages.

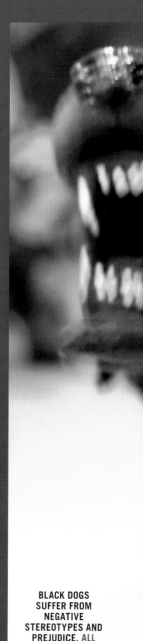

BLACK DOGS SUFFER FROM NEGATIVE STEREOTYPES AND PREJUDICE. ALL UNDESERVED, OF COURSE.

ARE DOGS GOD?
OR JUST GODLIKE?

EXACTLY HOW AMAZING CAN DOGS BE? YOU TELL US

Okay, even if you don't believe dogs are god, everyone knows that they can be pretty amazing sometimes. How amazing? Take this quiz and see whether you're as amazing as the average pooch.

QUIZ

1. What brave act made Roselle a hero dog?

a. Roselle led Navy SEALs to Osama bin Laden's hiding place.

b. Roselle fought off pirates who tried to board Kanye's yacht off the coast of Kenya.

c. Roselle led her blind owner down 1,463 stairs to escape from the World Trade Center during September 11 attacks.

2. Dogs can predict what thirty to forty-five seconds before they happen?

a. Orgasms.

b. Earthquakes.

c. Epileptic seizures.

3. Dogs can be trained to sniff out what?

a. Pregnancy.

b. Cancer.

c. Pregnancy, cancer, and whether you've been sneaking chocolate chip cookies.

4. Dog fur helped how in what natural disaster?

a. It prevented Gulf of Mexico oil spill from spreading.

b. It shielded Japanese atomic plant workers from radiation following the 2011 earthquake.

c. It kept the trapped Chilean miners warm.

5. A dog survived the Asian tsunami floating for three weeks on what?

a. A humpback whale.

b. His dead owner.

c. A pile of trash.

6. Officials in Maryland and Virginia use dogs to find what hidden in state prisons?

a. Drugs.

b. Cell phones.

c. Innocent prisoners.

7. What breed of dog led police to a teenager trapped in a burning building?

a. Pit bull.

b. Saint Bernard.

c. Toy Poodle.

8. A recent study found that dogs can learn to perform simple what?

a. Household chores, such as bed making and toilet cleaning.

b. Nursing duties, such as bandage changing and bedpan emptying.

c. Math, such as addition and subtraction.

9. Missouri prison inmates taught a deaf dachshund what?

a. To act as a lookout while they dug an escape tunnel.

b. To hear.

c. Sign language.

10. British police officers had to learn what in order to communicate with their new Alsatian police dogs?

a. Sign language.

b. German.

c. To bark.

CRAZY about your dog		Just CRAZY
Attending the Blessing of the Animals at your local church or temple.	▶	Choosing your religion based on its dog friendliness.
You believe you can communicate with your dog nonverbally.	▶	You believe your dog knows everything you're thinking, feeling, doing.
Hoping that if there's a heaven your dog gets to go there, too.	▶	Thinking your dog has a better chance of going to heaven than your mother, your child, or your priest.

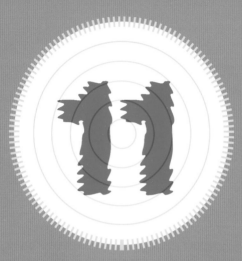

DEAD
DOGS

Is This Goodbye?
Or Just, See Ya Later?

It's not only in life that we obsess about our dogs. Dead dogs breed their own brand of mania.

While the death of celebrity dogs like Miss Ellie, the Chinese crested hairless who held the title of World's Ugliest Dog, can inspire their hometowns to name a day in their honor—as Pigeon Forge, Tennessee, did for Miss Ellie—the passing of more ordinary canines can also make their owners do extraordinary things.

Some things people do after their beloved pet has died, often to kinda pretend the dog hasn't died:

Taxidermy: While commemorative dog portraits were common in nineteenth-century England and France, having your dog stuffed and mounted has always been considered eccentric. Famous dogs such as Owney the postal dog and Balto the sled dog were routinely stuffed for display a hundred years ago. But these days taxidermy is, you'll pardon the expression, a dying art, and most taxidermists shy away from stuffing pets. The problem isn't squeamishness so much as how hard it is to satisfy the bereaved. It's difficult to bring the appropriate personality to a pet, taxidermists say, and so to make it look lifelike.

Mummification: A religious cult called Summum in Salt Lake City will mummify your dog much the same way the ancient Egyptians did, by removing its organs, immersing it in chemical preservatives for ten weeks, washing it, wrapping it in cotton gauze protected by a polyurethane membrane (okay, the Egyptians didn't have that), and then encasing it in a custom-made sarcophagus.

Freeze-drying: If you want to preserve your pet but can't find a taxidermist to accommodate you, Perpetual Pet offers an alternative: freeze-drying. Freeze-drying is a combination of freezing and drying: the dog is posed, ideally in a sleeping (i.e., kinda dead) position as that will look the most realistic. Then the body is frozen while at the same time moisture is extracted *veeeeeeeery slooooooooowly*. The process takes fifteen weeks for a Chihuahua, up to six months for a St. Bernard.

Sending them straight to heaven: For $110, a group called Eternal Earth-Bound Pets ensures that if the Rapture occurs within ten years of buying their policy, one dog per household will be saved rather than left behind on earth.

FOR HARDCORE REALISTS . . .

Those who've accepted that their dogs have died can try the following:

Virtual mourning: Several websites offer support groups, chat rooms, and other resources for dealing with your dog's passing.

Traditional funeral: Traditionalists can throw a funeral for their dog at an animal funeral home and cemetery, complete with coffin (available on Amazon), viewing, memorial service with religious readings, and burial with tombstone.

Cremation: As with humans, an increasing number of dogs are cremated today. Of course cremains can be buried or kept in an urn. But there may be more creative options.

NOTHING KILLS A DOG'S JUBILANT SPIRIT, **NOT EVEN DEATH.**

TEN THINGS TO DO WITH YOUR DOG'S ASHES (BESIDES BURY THEM IN THE BACKYARD)

Jane Fonda mistook her dear departed dog's ashes for bath salts, only realizing her mistake when she found pieces of bone floating in her nice hot tub. So what did she do? She went ahead with the bath, enjoying the sensation of being one with her dog.

Which is kind of horrifying, until you consider the alternatives. Go at the tub with a thousand tiny strainers, hoping to salvage the cremains? Just let the ashes go down the drain?

Accidentally bathing in your dog's ashes is better than accidentally snorting them, which two burglars in Florida did upon encountering an urn full of enticing white powder. Or smoking them, which more than one misguided dog lover on the Internet has been stupid enough to contemplate (and then stupid enough to talk about).

The following are all possible uses for your dog's ashes:

1. Hang them around your neck. Your pet's ashes can be cast into a gold, dog-shaped ring or necklace to make an item of what the manufacturer calls "wearable grief."

2. Wear them in your ears. Your dog's ashes can be turned into not-quite-real diamonds, which can then be turned into jewelry.

3. Paint with them. Use paint mixed with ashes to create a portrait of your dog.

4. Get inked with them. Ashes can be mixed with tattoo ink.

5. Stick some flowers in them. A perfume bottle, vase, or walking stick top can be made from art glass mixed with your dog's ashes.

6. Play tennis with them. You can have an art tennis ball made from your dog's favorite slobbery old tennis ball, your dog's ashes, and, uh, glass.

7. Dance to them. Press your dog's ashes into a vinyl record, maybe of his favorite songs?

8. Hug them. You can have your pet's ashes sewn into a pillow to make a "huggable urn."

9. Shoot them off as fireworks. The cremains are loaded into fireworks and shot off from a yacht at sea. Yacht extra.

10. Launch them into space. For $1,000 and up, Celestis Memorial Spaceflights will send your pet's cremains to the moon, and even back.

CRAZY? Sorry, God, But That's a Twisted Plan

Hundreds of people around the country rushed to adopt Daniel, a Beagle mix who survived the gas chamber at an Alabama shelter. On how Daniel managed to become only the third dog ever to cheat death at the Florence, Alabama, facility, a city spokesman posited, "Maybe God just had a better plan for this one." Next step in the divine plan: fly to Nutley, New Jersey, where Daniel is adopted into a home perhaps chosen by God himself.

HOW TO CLONE YOUR DOG . . .
IN TEN EASY STEPS (OR LESS!)

Peter Onruang spent more than $300,000 to clone his own dogs and wants to help you clone yours too. His site My Friend Again— myfriendagain.com—offers step-by-step instructions, which inspired this guide.

1. Think ahead! While the dog you want to have cloned is still alive, have your vet extract tissue and cells via a $1,500 biopsy kit from the firm ViaGen.

2. You didn't think ahead, did you? You waited until your dog died, didn't you? And now you're sitting there crying and missing her and wishing you could have her back. Wishing you'd spent the fifteen hundred bucks and gotten those cells so that you could now make yourself a new dog exactly like the dog you just lost. Well, it may not be too late! If your dog has been dead less than five days, you may still be able to extract clone-worthy biomatter. Go back to Step 1 and try again.

3. If your dog has been dead more than five days? Read Stephen King's *Pet Sematary.*

4. Get $100,000. No, I can't tell you how or where.

5. Send $100,000 and the cells from the dog you want cloned to RNL Bio in Seoul, South Korea. RNL Bio, affiliated with both Seoul National University and the South Korean government, has had dog-cloning successes and is the only company currently offering commercial pet cloning. Or, if that makes you too nervous, just send it all to me and I'll take care of everything. I swear I will.

6. Get an egg from a donor dog. Easier said than done; in fact, this—not the money, not the actual cloning part—can be the most difficult step in the process, given that dogs go into estrus only twice a year and produce a mere eight or so eggs at a time. The egg issue is why cloning is done most easily in Korea, where dog farms can supply both eggs and, you know, stew meat.

7. Replace the nucleus of the donor egg with the nucleus of the cell from your dog. Or at least have faith that someone else is doing this, along with zapping the cells with 3 to 7 volts of electricity and implanting them in a surrogate dog mother. Yeah, this is the part that makes it not just high-tech dog reproduction but actual cloning.

8. Wait six months to a year. This is for all the steps to be successful and your actual clone puppy to be born.

9. Wait two more months. Now you're waiting for the dog to get old enough to travel. Or maybe for those people who took your hundred grand to find a puppy who looks enough like your old dog to fool you.

10. Fly to Korea to pick up your new/old dog. And no, that is not included in the $100,000. And while your new dog should look pretty much like the one she was cloned from, scientists caution that she won't necessarily act like the original. It all goes back to nature vs. nurture: identical genes explain only part of the personality puzzle.

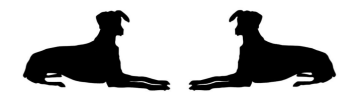

CRAZY about your dog		Just CRAZY
Feeling broken up when your dog dies.	▶	Feeling so broken up that you have his face tattooed on your chest.
Scattering your dog's ashes in his favorite park.	▶	Having your dog stuffed and mounted.
Wanting to get another dog just like the one you lost.	▶	Dog cloning.

ARE YOU CRAZY ABOUT YOUR DOG— OR JUST CRAZY?

Sure, you love your mutt. But how much puppy love is too much? Is your dog your best friend—or something disturbingly more?

Take this simple quiz to find out whether you're crazy about your dog—or just crazy.

1. You love your dog more than:
a. Your goldfish.
b. Your friends.
c. Your husband and kids.
d. Yourself.

2. What do you feed your dog?
a. The best dog food you can afford.
b. Burger, served in a specially monogrammed dish.
c. Filet mignon, which you feed him using a silver fork.
d. It depends on what restaurant the two of you are going to that night.

3. Top reason you like owning a dog:
a. Gives you someone to play catch with.
b. Gives you someone to talk to.
c. Gives you someone to sleep with.
d. Gives you someone to leave all your money to.

4. Wait, wait, wait—back to that "sleep with" part. When you say you sleep with your dog, what do you mean?

a. You sleep in the same room, the dog in his bed, you in yours.

b. The dog sleeps at the foot of your bed.

c. The dog sleeps in your bed, under the covers, his head on one pillow, yours on the other.

d. Yes, okay, it means what everybody thinks it means!!

5. Okay! So, when do you think being crazy about your dog crosses the line into craziness?

a. Carrying your dog with you everywhere you go, like Paris Hilton—that's crazy.

b. Dressing your dog in a raincoat and rubber booties when it's wet outside—that's crazy.

c. Marrying your dog like that guy in India did—that's crazy.

d. Crazy? Preferring people to dogs—that's crazy.

Key: If you answered mostly *a*'s, you're just a run-of-the-mill dog nut. Not any crazier than the rest of us.

If you answered mostly *b*'s, you're one of those people who talk about your dog at parties and create a Facebook page for him. Kinda crazy.

If you answered mostly *c*'s, I hate to tell you, but your house reeks of dog and you stopped noticing last Halloween. Yeah, you're pretty much out of your mind.

If you answered mostly *d*'s, what's your location, exactly? Because I'm sending some people in little white coats to pick you up.

Acknowledgments

My first thanks have to go to my son Joe Satran, whose idea this book may have been, and whose idea its title *definitely* was. Thanks, Joe, for letting me feast on the crumbs of your brilliance.

It has been my great pleasure to have written not one but two books with the wonderful editor Nancy Miller, friend of my youth and colleague of my—well, we'll call this later youth. Nancy and I had so much fun working together on *How Not to Act Old* that we had to come up with another joint project, and it was thrilling that she loved *Rabid* as much as I did.

Nancy's assistant, Lea Beresford, was another old acquaintance happily rediscovered on this project; thanks, Lea, for pulling everything together and making this book even more fun to work on than it had a right to be.

Thank you to my agent, Melissa Flashman, at Trident Media for so expertly making sure the project came together, and for laughing in all the encouraging places.

I had help researching everything from dog spa treatments to canine cloning from my insightful and hardworking research assistants Gianna Palmer, Jonah Comstock, Sonia Tsuruoka, Sara Kornhauser, and Joe Satran.

It was such a delight and a revelation to discover so many wonderful photographers and artists who contributed their work to making this book come alive. I would like to extend special thanks to Holly Wilmeth, who introduced me to Dan Borris, whose amazing Yoga Dogz not only set a high standard but made me believe I could meet it. And to the inspired artist John Fleenor, who recreated his hilarious and beautiful horoscope dogs in living color expressly for *Rabid*.

Thanks and love as always to friends and family who encouraged, analyzed, applauded, and simply were interested in this book:

Rita DiMatteo, Alice Elliott Dark, Louise DeSalvo, Liza Dawson, Christina Baker Kline, Laurie Albanese, Linda Rosenkrantz Finch, Hugh Hunter, Rory Satran, Nathaniel Kilcer, Owen Satran, and Dick Satran.

A NOTE ON THE AUTHOR

Pamela Redmond Satran is the author of the *New York Times* bestselling humor book *How Not to Act Old*, optioned by Amblin Entertainment. She is also the author of seven novels, most recently *The Possibility of You*, and a creator of the website Nameberry. A columnist for *Glamour*, Satran contributes frequently to such publications as the *Daily Beast*, the *Huffington Post*, and *More* magazine. Visit her website at pamelaredmondsatran.com.